Complex Litigation Confronts the Jury System:
A Case Study

Complex Litigation Confronts the Jury System: A Case Study

Arthur D. Austin

Edgar A. Hahn Professor of Jurisprudence
Case Western Reserve University

University Publications of America, Inc.

University Publications of America, Inc.
44 North Market Street, Frederick, Maryland 21701

Copyright © 1984 by Arthur D. Austin
All rights reserved

Library of Congress Cataloging in Publication Data

Austin, Arthur D.
  Complex litigation confronts the jury system.

  1. Jury—United States. 2. Complex litigation—
United States. 3. Antitrust law—United States.
I. Title.
KF8972.A95 1984   347.73'752   84-19500
ISBN 0-89093-484-3   347.307752

Printed in the United States of America

Contents

Preface vii

Part I
Introduction 1
The Right to Jury and Complex Litigation 3
Jury Comprehension 8
The Present Study: A Blend of Techniques 11

Part II
Introduction 21
Historical Context of the Litigation 23
The Substantive Issues 26
Jury Profiles 30
Trial I 32
The Miller Incident 36
Deliberation: Trial I 39
Trial II 43
Instructions 55

Part III
Introduction: Defining and Predicting Complexity 77
Fact-finding by the Jury in Antitrust Litigation 80
Static in the Fact-finding Process 87
Is Reliable Prediction of Complexity Possible? 95
Conclusions and Recommendations 99
Final Comments 105

Preface

On a cloudy day in mid-September of 1981, I took advantage of a break in my class schedule to attend the opening session of the *City of Cleveland* v. *Cleveland Electric Illuminating Co.* trial. On July 1, 1975, the city sued the rival of its municipal electric utility for monopolizing in violation of the Sherman Antitrust Act. The opening statements of counsel were impressive exhibitions of advocacy—they were well organized and persuasively presented. There was, however, one glaring deficiency: it would have taken an antitrust expert to understand what the lawyers were talking about.

Antitrust is a complicated area of the law. The statutes are ambiguous, nourishing sweeping interpretive latitude. The decisions are analytically convoluted and substantively contradictory. Lawyers have made money and academics have achieved tenure by arguing over the proper objectives and the correct interpretations of antitrust. The cases typically involve large business enterprises and millions of dollars ride on the outcome. Analogized to warfare, litigation is lengthy, costly, tedious, and complicated.

Complex litigation—antitrust warfare—challenges the credibility of the jury system. There is increasing doubt as to whether a typical jury can comprehend sufficiently to render a rational verdict.

As I watched the jurors staring expressionless at counsel as they sought to explain their cases in the hour and a half allocated to each side, I decided to use *Cleveland* v. *CEI* as a vehicle to study the problem of jury comprehension. From this point I was hooked and attended trial sessions as frequently as possible, speculating with counsel and spectators as to the jury's reaction to witnesses and evidence. Fortunately for my purposes, the first trial ended with a hung jury, resulting in a second trial and the opportunity to survey a different group of people. Moreover, the second jury held for the defendant while Jury I voted 5-1 in favor of the city. This gave me the unique chance to compare two juries who had different perceptions of the same evidence. It was also an opportunity to evaluate the impact of changes in trial tactics on jury comprehension.

For over two years I talked to jurors, lawyers, participants, reporters, and the judge. With few exceptions, they were enthusiastically helpful and extremely informative. In particular, the jurors were generous with their time and always candid in their comments. I am also grateful to Mr. Sam Miller, of Forest City Enterprises, who arranged a grant through the Jewish Federation of Cleveland. Dean Lindsey Cowen also provided support. As always, my good friend and mentor, Oscar Bealing, Esq., made valuable contributions throughout the process of research and writing.

Part I
Introduction

The existence of complex litigation is generating controversy over the ability of the jury system to function as an effective conflicts resolution mechanism. At issue is the capacity of jurors to comprehend complicated evidence sufficiently to render a rational decision. Chief Justice Burger has expressed doubts over the ability of the jury to adapt to the burden:

> It borders on cruelty to draft people to sit for long periods trying to cope with issues largely beyond their grasp.... Even Jefferson would be appalled at the prospect of a dozen of his yeomen and artisans trying to cope with some of today's complex litigation in trials lasting many weeks or months.[1]

The Chief Justice's opinion does not, by any means, represent a consensus: the scholars[2] are divided on the question, as are the Third and Ninth Circuits. The Ninth Circuit refused to accept the possibility of any case being "so overwhelmingly complex that it is beyond the abilities of a jury."[3] The Third Circuit disagreed, holding that "due process precludes trial by jury when a jury is unable to perform [its] task with a reasonable understanding of the evidence and legal rules."[4]

Complex litigation is the product of the friction between the adversarial legal system and a postindustrial society. Today's economic environment is characterized by rapidly evolving technology and science-intensive industries. The new competition is in information, theory, and ideas. As a consequence, "the amount of knowledge is increasing at an exponential rate."[5] The most efficient method of responding to the constant eruption of technology is to fragment knowledge into narrow and manageable specialties. Each specialty communicates in its own arcane vernacular that defies translation into an everyman's language.

Hence even under ideal conditions, a jury will experience difficulty in comprehending evidence in litigation involving technologically intensive industries. But the adversarial system and its "exaggerated contentious procedure"[6] does not provide an ideal forum for education. A system that relies on contention encourages the use of stratagems to denigrate opponents while seeking to enhance the credibility of the client. As a result, facts, already mysterious to the nonspecialist, are often obscured in the advocacy style and acting ability of counsel.

Competing with lawyers in the art of persuasion are expert witnesses, hired for bias and communication skills. As the elite of the technological age because of access to the various subsystems of knowledge, experts are the lifeblood of complex litigation.[7] As specialists, they contribute abstruse testimony—and obfuscation.

Two innovations of the adversarial system—pervasive discovery and the class action—further aggravate the problem by lengthening the time of litigation. Discovery is time consuming—especially when its dragnet (the collection of voluminous documents) encourages obsessive overpreparation, a dedication to minutiae, and a tendency to file "shotgun" allegations.[8] Consolidating myriad litigants and lawyers into a single action under the class action motion renders trial management difficult and time consuming.[9]

Complex litigation has created a crisis in which, according to the press, "Juries Are On Trial."[10] Controversy and debate focus on two issues: (1) the constitutional law issue of whether the Seventh Amendment's preservation of a jury trial is absolute and hence does not countenance a complex litigation limitation, and (2) at what point litigation becomes too complex for a jury to render a rational verdict.

Resolution of the constitutional issue requires interpretation of legal history and the decisions. Although the Supreme Court has yet to make a judgment on the existing conflict between the Third and Ninth Circuits, scholars have provided ample advice and analysis.[11] On the other hand, determination of the capacity of the jury to comprehend complex litigation is a question of factual inquiry. Although there is extensive research on various aspects of jury behavior,[12] there is a paucity of empirical research on jury comprehension.

This study presents empirical data on jury comprehension. Part I presents an overview of the problem and describes the methodology of the study. Part II is research and analysis of two juries who participated in an antitrust trial. Part III evaluates Part II, reaches conclusions on jury comprehension, and considers the possible efficacy of comprehension improvement techniques.

The Right to Jury and Complex Litigation

1. Functions of the Jury

According to the Seventh Amendment, "[I]n suits at common law, where the value in controversy shall exceed twenty dollars, the right of trial by jury shall be preserved...."[13] This constitutional guarantee preserved jury rights existing in England at the time of the amendment's enactment (1791) and ensures a jury trial in legal—but not equitable—actions.[14] Described as "an exciting and gallant experiment in the conduct of human affairs,"[15] the jury system has survived controversy and attack to become firmly established as a fundamental right.

Supporters point to a congeries of justifications for preserving the right to a jury. It is argued, for example, that juries exercise a protective function by insulating litigants from biased or corrupt judges and thereby deflect political influence or the advantage of deep-pocket financial resources from the courtroom.[16] In channeling community values into the legal system, the jury also serves as a check on the possible excesses of the legislative branch.[17] A synergetic effect of group decision-making is assumed; "a jury as a group has wisdom and strength which need not characterize any of its individual members."[18] Another perceived virtue is the jury's ability to deliver black box decisions that, although arbitrary and irrational, do justice in special circumstances, but because unexplained, never become binding precedent.[19]

The jury's primary function, however, is to serve as the state's factfinder. This requires an impartial panel and the opportunity to hear, see, and comprehend all of the relevant evidence and testimony.[20] Controversies of fact are to be resolved in accordance wtih the court's instructions. According to the Supreme Court, "Jurors are supposed to reach their conclusions on the basis of common sense, common understanding and fair beliefs, grounded on evidence consisting of direct statements by witnesses or proof of circumstances from which inferences can fairly be drawn."[21]

Critics have over the years persistently expressed skepticism over reliable fact-finding by "12 persons brought in from the street, selected in various ways, for their lack of general ability...."[22] A conspicuous number of courts have now implicitly accepted this criticism by striking juries when confronted with complex litigation.

2. Justification for Granting a Motion to Strike a Jury

Speaking of the Seventh Amendment's preservation of the right to a jury for suits at common law, Justice Story said: "Beyond all question, the common law here alluded to is not the common law of any individual state (for it probably differs in all), but it is the common law of England, the grand reservoir of all our jurisprudence."[23] Accepting Story's premise, courts utilized the historical test; if the suit was legal as of 1791 under English common law, or if created subsequently it had an analogue at law, the guarantee of the Seventh Amendment was applicable.[24]

The stimulus for the complexity limitation is derived from the 1970 Supreme Court decision, *Ross* v. *Bernhard*, in which Justice White added some controversial language in footnote 10:

> As our cases indicate, the "legal" nature of an issue is determined by considering, first, the pre-merger custom with reference to such questions; second, the remedy sought; and, third, the practical abilities and limitations of juries.[25]

a. Bernstein

Footnote 10 has produced two rationales for dispensing with the jury. In *Bernstein* v. *Universal Pictures, Inc.*,[26] the district court subsumed the third prong of footnote 10 under the traditional power of equity to evaluate the adequacy of the legal remedy in determining jurisdiction. If the remedy sought (prong two) involves complexities, equity must necessarily consider the "practical abilities and limitation of juries" in determining the adequacy of the legal remedy. And it follows that "the adequacy of the legal remedy necessarily involves the adequacy of the jury and its competency to find the facts."[27] Where the jury is incapable of handling complex litigation, thereby inhibiting realization of an effective legal remedy, equity has the power "to strike a jury demand when to allow it to stand would work an injustice."[28]

Bernstein feeds controversy into the historical test. Devlin argues that it was part of the "accepted relationship between equity and common law"[29] for the chancellor to stop an action at law where the jury could not cope with complexities, while Arnold argues that such a view is "without general support"[30] in English legal history. Jorde advances a third analysis; the historical approach requires a determination of those issues decided by law and equity in 1791. "Only for those issues tried to juries in 1791 is the right to jury trial preserved by the Seventh Amendment."[31] He concludes that English juries heard and decided analogous antitrust conduct and damage issues but not a market structure counterpart. He would, therefore, allow the removal of structural questions like market definition and market share from the jury.

b. *The Due Process Limitation*

In the cryptic opinion of *In re Boise Cascade Securities Lit.*,[32] a district court held that the third prong of footnote 10 is of "constitutional dimensions"[33] and serves as a limitation to the Seventh Amendment. Accordingly, when litigation exceeds the capacity of the jury to "decide the facts in an informed and capable manner,"[34] there is no Seventh Amendment guarantee.

The due process guarantee was expressly recognized in *In re Japanese Elect. Prod. Antitrust Lit.*, where the Third Circuit conceded the inappropriateness of reading too much into the third prong but nevertheless concluded that the Supreme Court left open the possibility that jury incompetence "may limit the range of suits subject to the seventh amendment and has read its prior seventh amendment decisions as not precluding such a ruling."[36] Capitalizing on this preface, the court held that a jury unable to perform its responsibilities infringes due process, justifying a limitation on the Seventh Amendment.

According to the Third Circuit, a jury incapable of rendering a rational verdict subverts due process in three ways: (1) legal remedies may be rendered which are inconsistent with the objectives of the laws; (2) the likelihood of unpredictable verdicts is increased; and (3) "unless the jury can understand the evidence and the legal rules sufficiently to rest its decision on them, the objective of most rules of evidence and procedure in promoting a fair trial will be lost entirely."[37]

3. *Motion to Strike: Burden of Proof*

Assuming that the constitutional issue is resolved in favor of a complex litigation limitation on the Seventh Amendment, the factual issue of identifying complexity must be confronted. Consistent with the strong imprimatur of the Seventh Amendment, a successful motion to strike must satisfy a high burden of proof.[38] Hence, it is "only in exceptional"[39] cases that a court will strike a jury. Moreover, *Bernstein* and *In re Japanese Elect. Prod. Antitrust Lit.* require proof that the case cannot be rendered comprehensible by the use of special trial techniques such as special master and the other clarifying procedures recommended in the Manual for Complex Litigation.[40]

Must the party making the motion offer proof that the court is capable of comprehending the litigation? The court in *Boise* observed that identifying jury limitations "does not answer the problems ... unless it can be shown that trial to the Court would be superior."[41] The Third Circuit held that a "general presumption" of the court's capability "is reasonable."[42] Both courts described the judiciary's advantages: the judge can utilize experience to identify the issues, separate the relevant from the superfluous, translate and distill expert testimony, and correctly apply legal standards. In addition, a judge can review transcripts daily and, unlike a jury, is under no pressure to render an immediate verdict. A judge can also reopen the trial to obtain new evidence or clarification.[43] An important advantage in complex litigation is the judge's decision to utilize court appointed specialists—such as economists—to explain and educate.[44]

Cases refusing to recognize a complex litigation limitation on the Seventh Amendment deny that a judge is superior to a jury. In conclusory terms, the Ninth Circuit stated that "no one has yet demonstrated how one judge can be a superior fact-finder to the knowledge and experience that citizens-jurors bring to bear on a case."[45] In *Zenith Radio Corp.* v. *Matsushita Elec. Industrial Co.*,[46] Judge Becker described reasons for the jury's superiority over a judge: a jury disciplines lawyers into adopting efficient trial techniques and methods of enhancing communication. A judge does not have the advantage of the collective experience and interaction of a jury, an asset that gives the latter an edge in tasks such as evaluating the credibility of witnesses.[47] Judge Becker also rejected the assumption that a judge will necessarily possess superior education or qualification, observing that "one is more likely to find a computer technician or an economist in a jury than on the bench."[48]

4. Identifying Complex Litigation

"[T]he point at which a jury's limitation exceeds its abilities is not precise nor is it easy of definition."[49] Generally, the court has the task of examining the allegations in the context of an inchoate record, reviewing the available exhibits, depositions, and witness lists, and then projecting the capacity of a hypothetical jury to comprehend.[50]

Although the courts have considered a cluster of factors in determining complexity, the length of the trial and the substantive depth of the allegations are of critical importance.[51] Projected length is estimated by reference to such factors as the number of litigants, witnesses, depositions, and exhibits. Length of the trial is thought to have a critical bearing on complexity for three reasons. First, a long trial produces a jury profile of housewives, retired people or otherwise available people whose employment requirements furnish the freedom to serve.[52] The result is a jury that does not constitute "a fair cross section of the community at large," and consequently "a basic purpose of the jury, the determination of facts by impartial minds of diverse backgrounds, is defeated if a sizable and significant portion of the community must be excluded from service."[53] Second, a concomitant effect is that a jury with this background would likely lack experience in commercial affairs and thus not be capable of understanding financial and business terminology.[54] Third, a long trial has a disabling effect on a jury, and "can interrupt the career and personal life of a jury member and thereby strain his commitment to the jury's task."[55]

The substantive range of the allegations determines the extent of the intellectual demands on the jury. Most of the complex litigation cases involve violations of securities or antitrust laws.[56] Antitrust presents the jury with a blend of legal, economic, and social policy doctrines. Enigmatic terms such as *cross-elasticity of demand, marginal revenue,* and *monopoly power* confound even the economists, who will appear as "hired gun" experts. The jury must understand conflicting testimony involving these concepts and then manipulate them within the parameters of legal definitions embodied in the instructions.[57]

The geographical and technological character of the firms and industries are relevant. A jury may experience difficulty in coping with the "cultural shock" of the methods of doing business by foreign firms and in understanding the customs of foreign markets.[58] Some industries, such as computers, involve sophisticated technology well beyond the comprehension of those without training. As the foreman of the *ILC Peripherals Leasing Corp.* v. *IBM Corp.* jury complained to the court: "If you can find a jury that's both a computer technician, a lawyer, an economist, knows all about that stuff, yes, I think you could have a qualified jury."[59]

Jury Comprehension

1. An A Priori Prediction

Under normal conditions, the court makes the judgment that the case is beyond the comprehension of a hypothetical jury. Since at this point in the proceedings there is no way that the judge can actually test the jurors' capacity to comprehend, the motion to strike is granted on the basis of an *a priori* prediction. Hence there presently exists a gap in knowledge as to what are the most reliable indicia of a jury's inability to comprehend. Thus far, this gap has been ignored,[60] or evaded by presuming the superiority of the judge.[61] The reason is a lack of substantive research. "Neither the social science community nor the legal profession has furnished the courts with the information needed for empirically grounded judgements about the capacity of juries to rationally decide the issues posed by complex civil suits."[62]

2. Reasons for Lack of Research

One obvious reason for the lack of empirical data is the relatively recent recognition of the issue. The first decision addressing the problem of jury comprehension, complex litigation, and the Seventh Amendment was decided in 1976.[63] Moreover, the opportunities for investigation are limited by the infrequency of complex litigation[64] and the preference of litigants, especially where the government is involved, to rely on nonjury trials. The government's actions against IBM[65] and AT&T,[66] both considered the ultimate stress on the judicial system and potentially a fertile source of study, were nonjury. Another inhibiting factor is the existence of court rules discouraging posttrial interviews of jurors.[67] Moreover, the logistics and the costs involved in contacting jurors and collecting information can be formidable.[68]

3. Methodology: Impediment to Understanding How Much a Jury Understands

The above problems are, however, insignificant in comparison with the major obstacle in researching jury comprehension: obtaining accurate and reliable information. Jury comprehension research involves quantification problems, and studies are vulnerable to various forms of "static," such as memory lapse, interviewer bias, and juror rationalization. There are at least three research methods, each with trade-offs of advantages and disadvantages.

a. Simulation

A jury selected with predetermined qualifications views video tapes of segments such as opening statements, expert testimony, and the instructions of a completed trial. The "jury" is then questioned either by personal interview or written examination to measure the level of comprehension.[69]

Since it is probable that the video tape would be an acted script of a real trial, it will lack the cutting edge of the live drama. A mock jury does not have the opportunity to develop the interaction synergy that educates and colors the thinking of a real jury. The influence of *ennui* and the fatigue of a long trial is filtered out. Moreover, the use of video slices of a trial artificially skews the attention of the jury toward the most significant portions of the case. On the other hand, "realistic simulation is impossible if realism requires evidence so voluminous that it takes months to present. Both the production cost of the required tape and the cost of acquiring subjects are likely to be prohibitive."[70]

b. Shadow Jury

By impaneling a jury that attends an ongoing trial, the shadow jury technique avoids some of the defects in simulation. The advantage of the shadow jury is that it is exposed to the full drama of an authentic trial, even entering and leaving the courtroom with the real jury during breaks and bench conferences. Daily debriefing seeks to ascertain cumulative and daily comprehension.[71]

However, since the shadow jurors do not have the responsibility to render a verdict, their attention span is suspect. Without the incentive to pay attention, the "difference between actual and shadow juries may become greater and greater as trials progress."[72] It is also doubtful whether jury interaction can blossom. The biggest defect is that daily or frequent debriefing emphasizes that the exercise is special and artificial, which may affect the juror's responses and may encourage commentary for the sake of participation. Finally, the cost factor may be prohibitive. IBM allocated $125,000 for its shadow jury.[73]

c. Personal Interviews

One of the most reliable techniques is to interview actual jurors immediately after they render a verdict.[74] The events of the trial are fresh, permitting the interviewer to ascertain the juror's perception of witnesses, key issues, and relevant terms. There are defects—some jurors may twist their responses to fit the verdict or seek to exaggerate their influence on deliberation. These are modest, however, compared to the value of firsthand impressions.

The major problem with the personal interview technique is that it is a difficult undertaking. Some jurors may refuse to cooperate. Interviewers may lack expertise; to conduct the survey properly, interviewers should have an in-depth understanding of the facts, law, and strategies. Constant observation of the trial is necessary in order to learn the idiosyncrasies of the lawyers and judge that may affect comprehension.

The Present Study: A Blend of Techniques

I conducted a study of jury comprehension of antitrust litigation in Cleveland, Ohio, and in the process used a blend of techniques in what can best be described as an eclectic approach. *City of Cleveland v. Cleveland Electric Illuminating Company (Cleve. v. CEI)*[75] provided a fertile research source: a publicly owned electrical utility charged its rival, an investor-owned utility, with violations of the antitrust laws. The suit was complicated by the existence of various federal and state regulations applicable to the defendant and by the defendant's argument that its behavior was legally permissible in a natural monopoly. Most importantly, the case provided the study with two juries: Trial I ended in a mistrial with the jury favoring the plaintiff 5-1, while Trial II resulted in a 6-0 verdict for the defendant.

The purpose of the study was to identify and evaluate those factors that may influence and affect jury comprehension. As I gained further insights from experience, the scope of the survey evolved and expanded to utilize the following techniques.

1. Observation

I attended Trial I approximately two or three times per week and Trial II on a regular, and at times on a daily, basis. These visits enabled me to observe the jury as it reacted to the presentation of evidence. Being able to see the jurors' response to the advocacy style of the lawyers, the rulings of the court, and critical testimony provided a rich and necessary background for subsequent interviews.

In order to develop a feel for the complexity problems encountered by the jurors,[76] I read daily transcripts, which were supplemented with frequent conversations with the lawyers.

2. Personal Interviews

a. Jury I

Trial I was declared a mistrial after the jury could not resolve a 5-1 vote favoring the plaintiff. The jury originally had six alternates but one was excused. The survey of Jury I was initiated with a written questionnaire requiring yes/no or short answers. The objective was to get a general impression of the jury's attitude, explain the purpose of the study, and to establish a bridge of familiarity for personal interviews. All eleven jurors and alternates responded. (Hereafter, *jurors* refers to voting members as distinguished from alternates.)

I interviewed five of the six jurors. (The remaining juror refused to return phone calls.) The foreman was interviewed at her home twice for approximately an hour and a half per interview and subsequently by phone interview. The dissenter was interviewed at her home (approximately one and a half hours) followed by two phone interviews lasting thirty to forty-five minutes each. Another juror who was active and influential in the deliberations was interviewed two times at his home, each visit lasting slightly over an hour. The two remaining jurors indicated a preference for phone interviews and were obliged, with each interview lasting approximately forty-five minutes.

Four of the five alternates were interviewed; two by personal visits and two by phone at their request. The length of interviews was forty-five minutes to an hour.

While the interview generally followed a prepared list of topics, jurors were allowed—and encouraged—to discuss any aspect of the trial. As a result, many observations were spontaneous. With the exception of an alternate who complained that the trial was a "bad experience," the jury was cooperative. They were friendly, candid, and willing to answer any question; the two central characters in the drama—foreman and dissenter—were especially helpful and informative.

b. Jury II

Two voting members of Jury II were not interviewed; one refused while the other made her disinclination evident by neither returning phone calls nor keeping appointments. The remaining four were successfully interviewed; three at home and one by phone. The home visits lasted around one and one quarter hours while the phone discussion was forty-five minutes to an hour long. Two jurors were subsequently interviewed for a second time by phone. Six of the seven alternates were interviewed, four in personal visits and two by phone at their request.[77] The one declining alternate expressed bitterness, complaining that the trial "was an experience that I don't want to go through again."

The next phase of contact with Jury II was a group discussion by the four cooperating jurors at Case Western Reserve University Law School. Through a seminar format, the jurors discussed numerous topics, including impressions of the witnesses, testimony, lawyers, and their thought processes during deliberation. The discussion lasted one and one quarter hours and was video taped. The group then had lunch while viewing the tapes and continued their commentary on the events of Trial II. This was a productive meeting since it provided the jury with an opportunity to reflect on the trial without the pressure of reaching a verdict and to exchange views on topics that had fallen within the court's admonition not to discuss the case during the trial.

Like Jury I, the members of Jury II who agreed to be interviewed were cooperative and candid. However, as will be discussed below, there were sharp differences between Juries I and II.

3. Instructions

The decisions have thus far not expressly identified instructions as a factor in jury comprehension. This is undoubtedly because the ruling on the motion to strike occurs at the threshold of the trial and it is thus too early for instructions to have been formulated beyond the tentative stage. Instructions are, however, of critical importance since the jury must be able to comprehend and apply legal rules in order to render a rational verdict.

The study evaluated the impact of instructions on jury comprehension in four ways: (1) instruction comprehension was a topic of the personal interviews, (2) instructions from both trials were evaluated by a specialist to determine the readability level, (3) the instructions were read to a jury of law students who were quizzed for comprehension, and (4) a psycholinguistic study was conducted to determine comprehensibility of instructions and to identify those portions causing the greatest static in comprehension.

Notes

1. New York L.J. Aug. 13, 1979, p. 21. See, *The Jury in Complex Litigation*, Judicature, Vol. 65, March-April, 1982.

2. The literature typically focuses on two issues, identification of complexity and whether there is a constitutional limitation on the right to jury granted by the Seventh Amendment. *See generally*: Lempert, *Civil Juries and Complex Cases: Let's Not Rush to Judgment*, 80 Mich. L. Rev. 68 (1981); Kuhlman, Pontilces, Stevens, *Jury Trial, Progress, and Democracy*, 14 J. Marshall L. Rev. 679 (1981); Jorde, *The Seventh Amendment Right to Jury Trial of Antitrust Issues*, 69 Calif. L. Rev. 1 (1981); Arnold, *A Historical Inquiry Into the Right to Trial by Jury in Complex Civil Litigation*, 128 U. Pa. L. Rev. 829 (1980); Campbell, LePoidevin, *Complex Cases and Jury Trials: A Reply to Professor Arnold*, 128 U. Pa. L. Rev. 965 (1980); Devlin, *Jury Trial of Complex Cases: English Practice at the Time of the Seventh Amendment*, 80 Colum. L. Rev. 43 (1980); Higginbotham, *Continuing the Dialogue: Civil Juries and the Allocation of Judicial Power*, 56 Tex. L. Rev. 47 (1977); Kane, *Civil Jury Trial: The Case for Reasoned Iconoclasm*, 28 Hastings L.J. 1 (1976); Redish, *Seventh Amendment Right to Jury Trial: A Study in the Irrationality of Rational Decision Making*, 70 Nw. U.L. Rev. 486 (1975); Wolfram, *The Constitutional History of the Seventh Amendment*, 57 Minn. L. Rev. 639 (1973).

3. In re U.S. Financial Securities Litigation, 609 F.2d 411, 432 (9th Cir. 1979).

4. In re Japanese Electronic Products Antitrust Lit., 631 F.2d 1069, 1084 (3d Cir. 1980).

5. D. Bell, The Post Industrial Society 177. *See also* J. Naisbitt, Megatrends (1982).

6. R. Pound, The Causes of Popular Dissatisfaction with the Administration of Justice, 29 ABA Rep. 395–417 (Part 1, 1906).

7. "The 'battle of experts' which attends the presentation of so many of our complex disputes is so common and so typical, as to have become the butt of crude humor—'How much did your expert cost?'." M. Wessel, Science and Conscience 45 (1980).

8. *See* P. Gerhart, *Report on the Empirical Case Studies Project*, to the National Commission for the Review of Antitrust Laws and Procedures 8-10 (1979).

9. *See* Manual for Complex Litigation (5th ed. 1982).
10. Time, Sept. 3, 1979, p. 61.
11. *See* note 2, *supra*.
12. The best known is the extensive study conducted by Kalven & Zeisel at the University of Chicago. *See* H. Kalven, H. Zeisel, The American Jury (1966).
13. U.S. Const. amend. VII.
14. Baltimore's Carolina Line, Inc. v. Redman, 245 U.S. 654, 659 (1935); Devlin, *supra* note 2 at 44, Jorde, *supra* note 2 at 7.
15. Kalven, *The Dignity of the Civil Jury*, 50 Va. L. Rev. 1055 (1964).
16. Wolfram, *supra* note 2 at 653. *See* Comment, *Jury Trials in Complex Litigation*, 53 St. John's L. Rev. 751, 753 (1979).
17. Wolfram, *supra* note 2 at 653.
18. Kalven, Zeisel, *supra* note 12 at 8.
19. Higginbotham, *supra* note 2 at 57. *See* G. Calabresi, F. Bobbitt, Tragic Choices 57–79 (1977).
20. "It is the jury, not the court, which is the fact-finding body. It weighs the contradictory evidence and references, judges the credibility of witnesses, receives expert instructions, and draws the ultimate conclusion as to the facts." Tennant v. Peoria & P.U. Ry. Co., 321 U.S. 29, 35 (1944).
21. Schulz v. Pennsylvania R. Co., 350 U.S. 523, 526 (1956).
22. Kalven, *supra* note 15 at 1068.
23. U.S. v. Wonson, 28 F. Cas. 745, 750 (C.C.D. Mass. 1812).
24. *See* Wolfram, *supra* note 2.
25. 396 U.S. 531, 538 n. 10 (1970).
26. 79 F.R.D. 59 (S.D.N.Y. 1978).
27. 79 F.R.D. at 66.
28. *Id*.
29. Devlin, *supra* note 2 at 107.
30. Arnold, *supra* note 2 at 830.
31. Jorde, *supra* note 2 at 9–10.
32. 420 F. Supp. 99 (W.D. Wash. 1976).
33. 420 F. Supp. at 105.
34. 420 F. Supp. at 104.
35. 631 F.2d 1069 (3d Cir. 1980).
36. 631 F.2d at 1080.
37. 631 F.2d at 1084.
38. "We do not believe that a due process limitation allows the district courts a substantial amount of discretion to deny jury trials. Because preservation of the right to jury trial remains a constitutionally protected interest, denials of jury trials on grounds of complexity should be confined to suits in which

due process clearly requires a nonjury trial. This implies a high standard. It is not enough that trial to the court would be preferable. The complexity of a suit must be so great that it renders the suit beyond the ability of a jury to decide by rational means with a reasonable understanding of the evidence and applicable legal rules." 631 F.2d at 1088.
39. 631 F.2d at 1089.
40. 631 F.2d at 1088; 79 F.R.D. at 70.
41. 420 F. Supp. at 104.
42. 631 F.2d at 1086–7.
43. *See* Comment, *The Right to Trial by Jury in Complex Litigation*, 20 Wm. & Mary L. Rev. 329, 353 (1978).
44. Perhaps the best known use of an economic expert was Judge Wyzanski's use of Harvard economist Carl Kaysen in U.S. v. United Shoe Mach. Corp., 110 F. Supp. 295 (D. Mass. 1953). *See* C. Kaysen, United States v. United Shoe Machinery Corporation (1956).
45. In re U.S. Financial Securities Litigation, 609 F.2d 411, 431 (9th Cir. 1979).
46. 1979-2 Trade Cas. 62753.
47. 1979-2 Trade Cas. 62753, at 78342.
48. *Id.*
49. 420 F. Supp. at 104.
50. A hung jury would provide the court with an opportunity to observe the jury, evaluate the complexity of evidence, and question the jurors on comprehension. This occurred in ILC Peripherals Leasing Corp. v. IBM Corp., 1978-2 Trade Cas. 62177, where Judge Conti granted IBM's motion to strike a jury, noting:

> Here...the court is able to base its decision on its own observations during the five-month trial.... Throughout the trial, the court felt that the jury was having trouble grasping the concepts that were being discussed by the expert witnesses, most of whom had doctorate degrees in their specialties. This perception was confirmed when the court questioned the jurors during the course of their deliberation and after they were discharged.

Id. at 75269.

See Comment, *The Seventh Amendment and Complex Civil Litigation: The Demise of the Complexity Exception to Trial by Jury and the Search for a Viable Due Process Alternative*, 50 Miss. L.J. 572 (1979); Comment, *The Right to Strike the Jury: Trial Demand in Complex Litigation*, 34 Miami L. Rev. 243 (1980); Note, *Preserving the Right to Jury Trial in Complex Civil Cases*, 32 Stan. L. Rev. 99 (1979); Comment, *The Right to a Jury Trial in Complex Litigation*, 92 Harv. L. Rev. 898 (1979).
51. "A suit might be excessively complex as a result of any set of circumstances which singly or in combination render a jury unable to decide in the foregoing rational manner. Examples of such circumstances are an exceptionally long trial period and conceptually difficult factual issues." 631 F.2d at 1079.

Notes

52. "When persons entitled to be excused from such a lengthy case have been eliminated from the venire, must litigants be left with a panel consisting solely of retired people, the idle rich, those on welfare, and housewives whose children are grown?" 79 F.R.D. at 70.

53. 420 F. Supp. at 104. See Comment, *The Right to an Incompetent Jury: Protracted Commercial Litigation and the Seventh Amendment*, 10 Conn. L. Rev. 775 (1978).

54. 420 F. Supp. at 104.

55. 631 F.2d at 1086.

56. In re Boise Cascade Securities Lit. (securities); Bernstein v. Universal Pictures, Inc. (antitrust); ILC Peripherals Leasing Corp. v. IBM (antitrust); In re Japanese Electronic Products Antitrust Lit. (antitrust, antidumping).

57. Evaluating the jury's competence after a hung jury, Judge Conti stated:

> While the Court was appreciative of the effort they put into deciding the case, it is understandable that people with such backgrounds would have trouble applying concepts like cross-elasticity of supply and demand, market share and market power, reverse engineering, product interface manipulation, discriminatory pricing, barriers to entry, exclusionary leasing, entrepreneurial subsidiaries, subordinated debentures, stock options, modeling, and etc.

ILC Peripherals Leasing Corp. v. IBM Corp., 1978-2 Trade Cas. 62177 at 75270.

58. *See* 631 F.2d at 1074.

59. 1982-2 Trade Cas. 62177 at 75270.

60. In re Boise Cascade Securities Lit., 420 F. Supp. 99 (W.D. Wash. 1976); Bernstein v. Universal Pictures, Inc., 79 F.R.D. 59 (S.D.N.Y. 1978).

61. 631 F.2d at 1086. Plaintiffs argued that the "hypothetical prospect" of a jury rendering an improper verdict "carries less weight than the preservation of the right to jury...." Judge Seitz responded:

> The due process objection does concern, to be sure, a possibility of an erroneous and erratic jury verdict that might not occur, but this possibility is anything but remote. If the jury is unable to understand the evidence and legal rules the possibility is substantial. Striking a jury trial demand in order to prevent this possibility is prospective relief. However, the procedural requirements of due process are by their very nature prospective: They are safeguards against the possibility of erroneous and arbitrary deprivations of liberty and property. This feature never has been thought to diminish their importance.

Id. at 1085.

62. Lempert, *supra* note 2 at 70-1. The Ninth Circuit observed: "Although various views have been expressed about the practical abilities of jurors, there has been little substantive research done on the subject." In re U.S. Financial Securities Lit., 609 F.2d 412, 420 (9th Cir. 1979).

63. In re Boise Cascade Securities Lit., 420 F. Supp. 99 (W.D. Wash. 1976).

64. "Protracted civil trials (defined here as lasting longer than 19 trial days or 100 trial hours) account for almost 12 percent of civil trial hours, even though they represent less than 1 percent of all civil trials. These trials are, therefore, a legitimate cause of concern to the judiciary." Protracted Civil Trials: Views from the Bench and Bar vii (Fed. Judicial Center 1981).

65. U.S. v. IBM, 69 Cir. 200-Div. No. 72-344 (D.N.Y.).

66. Discussed in *Complex Antitrust Cases: Need They Always Drag On?*, Antitrust Trade Reg. Rep., No. 786, AA-1, Oct. 26, 1976.

67. "No attorney connected with the trial of an action shall himself, or through any investigator or other person acting for him, interview, examine or question any juror with respect to the verdict or deliberations of the jury in action except with leave of court granted upon good cause shown." Rules for the United States District Court, Southern Dist. of Ohio § 5.5 (1981). The danger is that jurors will be harassed in an effort to uncover improper conduct to be used to support a motion to set aside a verdict. *See, Interviewing Jurors After Verdict* § 606[06] Weinstein's Evidence, Vol. 3 (1981). In controversial cases, jurors may be harassed by the media and thus be reluctant to talk to researchers. *See, The Juror As Celebrity*, Time, Aug. 16, 1982. In England it is illegal to question jurors. Cleveland Plain Dealer, Aug. 28, 1982, p. 2–13. *See generally*, Note, *Public Disclosures of Jury Deliberations*, 96 Harv. L. Rev. 886 (1983).

68. The author drove over 1,250 miles within a three-county area to interview jurors.

69. *See*, e.g., M. Saks, Jury Verdicts (1977); Hunt, *Putting Juries On the Couch*, N.Y. Times Magazine, Nov. 28, 1982, p. 70.

70. Lempert, *supra* note 2 at 100–01.

71. IBM is credited with originating the shadow jury. "In a highly unusual legal move, a major American corporation on trial in a $300 million civil suit has paid six ordinary citizens to act as a 'shadow' jury in the case. The job of the 'jurors' is to report on their impressions of testimony and lawyers' presentation after each courtroom day. These views are then made available to attorneys for the International Business Machines Corp., the defendant in the case.

"The purpose of the experiment is to give IBM's lawyers some inkling of how well the 12 actual jurors are absorbing the mounds of evidence in the wearisomely technical antitrust case and what their opinions of the trial might be." Chicago Tribune, Jan. 27, 1977, Se. 1, p. 5. When the actual jurors discovered the shadow jury, IBM discontinued its use. Wall St. J., April 3, 1981, § 2, p. 19. For a description of the IBM experience *see* Vinson, *The Shadow Jury: An Experiment in Litigation Science*, 68 A.B.A. L.J. 1242, Oct., 1982.

72. Lempert, *supra* note 2 at 99.

73. Wall St. J., Feb. 3, 1977, p. A 5.
74. Several surveys restricted interviews to judges and lawyers. Protracted Civil Trials: Views from the Bench and Bar (Fed. Judicial Center 1981); P. Gerhart, *Report On the Empirical Case Studies Project* to the Nat. Com. for the Review of Antitrust Laws and Procedures (1979). The information obtained is interesting, but hardly meaningful to the issue of juror competence.
75. City of Cleveland v. CEI, No. C75-560 (N.D. Ohio).
76. I agree with Lempert that familiarity with the record is necessary "for the intelligent implementation of other research strategies." Lempert, *supra* note 2 at 98.
77. Originally fourteen jurors were impaneled: six jurors and eight alternates. One alternate was excused for allegedly discussing the trial with a reporter. Cleveland Plain Dealer, Sept. 4, 1981, p. 1. The other alternate was excused near the end to take a planned vacation. The latter was interviewed, the former refused to discuss the trial.

Part II
Introduction

> It was a long trial, sometimes it was boring, sometimes it was really funny, sometimes it was downright silly. It was a good experience. I met a lot of nice people on the jury and we had a good time.
> —Alternate Juror, Trial II

> I never did feel that we knew everything anyway. I never felt that. I just felt, well, you know, here's one very shrewd lawyer taking one thing out of context and presenting it in this way and it sounds very reasonable and logical and here is another one taking the same, you know, thing out of context and presenting it with another view....
> —Alternate Juror, Trial II

On July 1, 1975, the city of Cleveland filed a complaint in federal district court alleging that the Cleveland Electric Illuminating Company (CEI) and four other electrical utilities had monopolized in violation of the Sherman Act.[1] On February 8, 1980, in exchange for $1.5 million and technical assistance, the plaintiff settled with all defendants except CEI.[2] The jury trial began with opening statements on September 15, 1980, in Judge Robert B. Krupansky's courtroom at the Federal Courthouse in Cleveland, Ohio.

On November 19, 1980, after thirteen days of deliberation, the judge declared a mistrial when the jury could not resolve a 5-1 vote favoring the city. Trial II began on July 13, 1981, and concluded on October 8, 1981, when the jury stunned and puzzled the public by deliberating less than six hours in reaching a verdict for CEI. In comparing the two results, a Cleveland newspaper editorialized that "the contrast with the first trial could not have been more marked."[3] Another local paper observed, "It has to be a puzzle to many how these jurors could arrive at such a quick decision after a long and complex trial involving so much technical evidence."[4]

The lawsuit produced a total juror universe of twenty-three perceptions of antitrust law and economics as filtered through the adversarial system.

Part II is an autopsy of the two trials from the perspectives of the jurors as they were exposed to the testimony and evidence. The descriptive analysis seeks to measure the significance and impact of the major components of litigation on jury comprehension. In the process, the behavior of the *Cleve. v. CEI* juries is compared with the accepted wisdom of various studies. Other factors, such as the impact of advocacy skills, the demeanor of the judge, and comprehensibility of instructions, are discussed. The initial section of Part II describes the allegations and history of *Cleve. v. CEI*.

Historical Context of the Litigation

1. Competition

The intense rivalry between the two electrical utilities dates back to the early 1900s when Cleveland annexed the villages of South Brooklyn and Collinwood and acquired their electric generating facilities.[5]

Competition immediately broke out between the Cleveland Municipal Electric Light and Power System ("Muny") and CEI, a private investor-owned utility serving the Cleveland area since the 1890s. Starting with 2,300 customers in 1910, Muny expanded its customer base to 23,000 by 1920.[6] By 1930, Muny serviced one-third of Cleveland and continued a modest growth during the depression years. In the late 1930s, the city moderated Muny's growth aspirations by adopting the yardstick policy.[7] Up to the late 1950s, Muny functioned as a type of shadow rate regulator for CEI by providing the public with a comparison as to price and service.[8] The Celebrezze administration terminated that yardstick policy, and by 1960 the two rivals were in direct competition along a thirty square mile area characterized by duplicate retail distribution facilities.[9] In the heated competition for customers and in response to what was perceived to be aggressive tactics, CEI adopted a free-wiring program—paying the cost of new internal wiring necessary for customers switching from Muny to CEI.

The most bitter conflict was over interconnection. Permanent synchronous interconnection permits instantaneous power transfers between two systems without interruption of customer service.[10] Other types of nonsynchronous power transfers, such as *dead load*, require disconnection and hence result in temporary interruption of customer service at the receiving end.[11]

Beginning in 1907, CEI provided Muny with dead load transfers during power emergencies. When Muny experienced major power outages in 1969, temporary nonsynchronous eleven kilovolt and sixty-nine kilovolt load transfer systems were constructed. In 1975, a permanent interconnection became operative under an order of the Federal Power Commission issued in 1973.[12] There is sharp disagreement over the events leading up to the interconnection.

CEI contended that it offered to interconnect during the 1960s, only to be rebuffed by city officials. According to the city, the offer was rejected because it was conditioned on the coercive limitation that Muny equalize its rates with CEI's prices. To CEI, this argument smoke-screened the real reason; the city feared that access to power would result in growing reliance on CEI and thereby undermine the independence that was necessary for Muny to operate either as a yardstick or as a viable competitor.[13]

The city argued that because Muny refused to capitulate to the rate equalization condition and thereby gain access to reliable power, it became vulnerable to a series of operational problems attributable to CEI. In power emergencies, for example, Muny could not obtain backup power instantaneously, but instead was forced to rely on dead load transfers which required interruption in service and resulted in "great inconvenience on Muny Light customers."[14]

During the Stokes administration in early 1970, Muny embarked upon a revitalization program which included efforts to obtain a synchronous interconnection with CEI.[15] The city's interpretation of the facts was that while agreeing in principle to the proposal, CEI resorted to various delaying ploys to inhibit actual installation.

Other incidents fueled the dispute. On February 18, 1971, CEI filed suit in Cuyahoga County Common Pleas Court seeking back payments for delivered load transfers of power. On May 13, 1971, the city filed a complaint with the Federal Power Commission requesting a permanent interconnection, an adjudication of the alleged arrearages, and an order precluding CEI from terminating load transfers. On May 21, 1971, CEI sought to terminate the load transfers by filing a Notice of Termination with the Federal Power Commission.[16] On January 11, 1973, the commission ordered the permanent interconnection.[17] In 1973, Muny became eligible for inexpensive power from the Power Authority of the State of New York (PASNY). Contending that it had no obligation to aid a rival, CEI refused the city's request to *wheel* (transmit) PASNY power over CEI's transmission lines.

2. Politics and Mismanagement

The conflicting philosophies of the tax-subsidized municipal system and the investor-owned CEI injected additional intensity into the rivalry.[18] Under the Utility Power Home Rule Amendments to the Ohio Constitution,[19] municipally operated utilities like Muny enjoy tax exemption benefits[20] and are excluded from the jurisdiction of the state rate-making system.[21] Moreover, the city can expand by acquiring utility facilities in various ways, including eminent domain.[22] As an investor-owned utility, CEI does not receive these benefits.

From its inception, Muny has been a hot political issue, serving as a lightning rod for praise and condemnation.[23] A highly vocal element extolled Muny as a beneficial institution for providing low cost electricity to the public. Critics charged that Muny was staffed by transitory management which impeded long-range planning, was burdened with incompetent patronage employees, and was vulnerable to the crosscurrents of political winds. In short, Muny was "an isolated, poorly designed and relatively unreliable system...[with] a history of inefficient operations."[24] The most vigorous allegations of mismanagement of Muny were, however, raised by CEI during the trials.

The Substantive Issues

1. Allegations

Alleging monopolization under Sherman section 2,[25] and seeking treble damages of $150 million,[26] the city vowed to prove that "CEI possesses monopoly power in the relevant market" and that CEI has "willfully maintained and expanded that market power."[27] Monopoly power, defined as "the power to control prices or exclude competition,"[28] was allegedly derived from three sources: (1) retail power in CEI's 1,700 square mile market or in the submarket of Cleveland, (2) wholesale power in the same two geographic markets, and (3) membership in the Central Area Power Coordination Group (CAPCO), a regional power exchange.[29] The court ruled that retail electrical power constituted the relevant product market and allowed the jury to determine the relevant geographic market.[30]

The defendants allegedly engaged in a "cluster" of acts, the "aggregate impact" of which evidenced "its willful maintenance of its monopoly."[31] The city identified the following cluster of monopolizing acts:

a. Refusal to Deal

Three forms of illegal refusals to deal were alleged: (1) the refusal to permit synchronous interconnection, thereby denying Muny access to retail power from CEI. Without backup power, Muny was vulnerable to emergencies such as power outages. Lack of backup power also prevented Muny from taking its generators off line for repairs and maintenance; (2) refusal to wheel PASNY power across CEI transmission lines, thereby cutting off an opportunity to obtain inexpensive power; (3) denial of access to the regional transmission grid. This prevented Muny from shopping around for low-priced power.

b. Predatory and Unfair Practices

Supplying free installation wiring to customers on condition that they buy CEI power (the Muny Displacement Program) and the making of "disparaging statements [to] potential customers of the City regarding the City's ability to offer reliable electrical services"[32] were characterized in

The Substantive Issues 27

the city's brief as "predatory and unfair." These actions were allegedly subsidized by CEI's deep pocket and were analogous to jumping market power from noncompetitive markets to inhibit rivals in competitive markets.[33]

c. The Miller Incident

The parties stipulated that Charles Miller, a Cleveland lawyer, was covertly hired by certain CEI officials to file a taxpayers' suit in Cuyahoga County Common Pleas Court seeking a temporary restraining order and injunction against the construction of the temporary emergency interconnection. The suit was subsequently dismissed.[34] The city alleged that the covert use of Miller was admissible as monopolizing or exclusionary conduct or as evidence of anticompetitive intention.[35]

d. Dirty Tricks

To establish exclusionary or anticompetitive intent and bolster its cluster theory, the city introduced evidence of alleged dirty tricks by CEI:

1. Rate equalization. CEI offered to interconnect but only on condition that Muny equalize rates. This evidenced two anticompetitive motives—price-fixing and paving the way to an easy acquisition of Muny.[36]
2. Muny surveillance. During the mid-1950s, CEI initiated a program of observing and monitoring Muny. Its objectives were, as a CEI executive testified, to ascertain "what their needs were, what the competitive situation was between their rates and our rates, their financial condition...the physical condition of their plant...."[37]
3. Bad faith negotiating. The city alleged that CEI failed to comply with the terms of an interconnection agreement and breached an offer to resolve a billing dispute.[38]
4. Terminated sale of maintenance power through load transfer, thereby making it impossible for Muny to make needed repairs.[39]
5. Engaged in delaying tactics after ordered to interconnect by the Federal Power Commission.[40]

e. Bottleneck Monopoly

The city isolated *bottleneck monopoly* as a distinct category of monopolization. The violation occurred upon CEI's refusal to grant Muny access to the bottleneck monopoly of its transmission lines. "CEI's transmission lines surrounding Muny Light's service area and separating Muny Light from other sources of power qualify as a bottleneck resource."[41]

2. The Defense

CEI adopted a two-pronged defense. Counsel employed aggressive cross-examination to contest the accuracy of the city's principal testimony regarding alleged anticompetitive behavior and intent. CEI also argued that its conduct was permissible as a matter of law.

a. Rationalization

Cross-examination and direct testimony were used to rationalize CEI's conduct as consistent with competition. The customer conversion program was presented as a rational response to a rival who used equally aggressive tactics. Rate equalization would have furnished Muny with power reliability. The refusal to wheel PASNY power was argued to be a rational business policy. "We will...wheel for you power that costs the same to you as it costs to us, but we feel that we do not have to give you the weapons to drive us out of business...."[42]

The dominant theme of the rationalization strategy was an attack on Muny's management.[43] Mismanagement accounted for the demise of the plaintiff's generating facilities, rendering it impossible to trace a proximate cause nexus between CEI's conduct and the alleged damages. Moreover, the alleged billing dispute and bad faith negotiations over interconnection were precipitated by incompetent Muny officials who lacked the necessary funding and wanted to engage in confrontation tactics.

b. Natural Monopoly

CEI argued that Sherman section 2 was irrelevant to the natural monopoly conditions of the Cleveland market. Section 2 is designed to prevent the maintenance or the willful exercise of market power in *competitive* markets. The goal is to maintain a competitive balance among rivals but nevertheless to recognize success when achieved by "superior skill, foresight and industry."[44] In a natural monopoly, where only one supplier can efficiently serve the market, these objectives are by definition unattainable:

> If such a market contains more than one firm, either the firm will quickly shake down to one through mergers or failures, or production will continue to consume more resources than necessary. In the first case competition is short-lived and in the second it produces inefficient results. Competition is thus not a viable regulatory mechanism under conditions of natural monopoly.[45]

If a newcomer invades a natural monopoly to engage in a struggle in which only one firm will survive, "the Sherman Act cannot be invoked either to prolong or police what is essentially a predatory struggle unrelated to the efficient allocation of resources which that Act is designed to foster."[46] While antitrust in inapplicable, the parties are not defenseless and can utilize other legal redress such as business tort, unfair trade practices, or the regulatory agencies.

c. Regulation of Investor-owned Utilities

CEI argued that pervasive public regulation of the investor-owned sector of the industry was relevant for two reasons: (1) An objective of regulation is to protect the public against the effects of wasteful competition in natural monopolies. The existence of regulation confirms that the market is a natural monopoly subject to the special antitrust treatment advocated by CEI. (2) The city's assertion that CEI possesses monopoly power—the predicate to monopolization—is undermined by pricing controls which inhibit CEI from exerting control over prices.[47]

Jury Profiles

And it has come to be well recognized generally that a litigant may get the best legal service obtainable; he may have, to many right thinking minds, the preponderance of testimony and right; but if his lawyers "can't pick a jury" his chances for success are very slim.[48]

Cleve. v. *CEI* was a highly publicized lawsuit. It was preceded literally by decades of publicity describing the status of the rivalry and the charges and countercharges by various officials. A proposed settlement of the suit, with the sale of Muny to CEI as a condition, the subsequent rejection of the proposed sale by Cleveland voters, along with Cleveland's near bankruptcy, were given extensive media attention and provided the pretrial atmosphere.[49]

1. Jury I Profile[50]

Jury I was blue collar; five had high school diplomas and one "attended" high school. Their employment background included two housewives, a postal worker, a retired welder, a temporary secretary, and a fish boner. With the exception of the twenty-six-year-old foreman, they were in the upper middle-aged range, averaging fifty-five years. Four jurors were CEI customers who expressed no service complaints, and all jurors indicated no prejudice against privately owned utilities. The other two jurors were served by utilities other than Muny. Three were from Cuyahoga County, which embraces Muny's service area, and three were from a contiguous county. Of the three Cuyahoga jurors, two opposed the proposed sale of Muny to CEI,[51] one of whom was the dissenter in the hung jury. Four jurors had some type of jury experience but only one, the dissenter, had been on a jury that went to a verdict.

2. Jury II Profile

As to education, Jury II was also blue collar; two had some high school experience, three received high school diplomas, and one had earned an associate degree from a community college. With two exceptions, the employment background could be considered above blue collar level: an auto assembly line supervisor, logistics support coordinator, customer affairs (credit) adjuster, and a department manager of a retail goods store. The other jurors were a housewife and a cook in a nursing home. (The value of the personal interview technique was demonstrated in the case of this juror. Despite her blue collar credentials, she was extremely articulate.) Moreover, Jury II was younger, averaging thirty-nine years of age. Five were serviced by CEI and one by Ohio Edison. They indicated no complaints or prejudices against private or public utilities. Only one juror, the foreman, had previous jury experience.

3. Comparison

The most discernable difference between the juries is the quality of work experience. Jury I was composed of lower-echelon blue collar workers whose jobs entailed very little, if any, decision-making responsibility. They performed at the end of the process, with no managerial opportunity. If the accepted strategy in jousting with a large enterprise is to select a blue collar jury, Jury I was a plaintiff's jury. In contrast, Jury II's work experience involved some degree of decision-making responsibility and the opportunity to exercise initiative. They were, therefore, a younger group with more of a management perspective.

Jury I presented a serious and somber demeanor while sitting through the trial. Sedately attentive, they seldom gazed at the audience, and once seated in the jury box, rarely conversed during bench conferences or other breaks.

Throughout the trial, Jury II openly and frequently expressed their reactions with smiles and frowns of doubt, amusement, or disapproval. During bench conferences between the court and lawyers, they often engaged in whispered conversation, at one time incurring the chastisement of the judge. They appeared to enjoy spirited combat between the lawyers and witnesses, sometimes exchanging glances and grins after a particularly robust confrontation.

The juries had one common trait: they were conscientious about their responsibilities and exhibited positive feelings about what they considered to be an important trial. The five jurors of Jury I were confident that but for the holdout, they would have rendered a correct verdict. (The dissenter was just as certain of her position.) Jury II was equally confident in the credibility of their verdict.

Jurors and alternates of each jury were essentially fungible as to age, employment, and educational characteristics. With the exception of one alternate from each jury who would have voted against the majority, the views of alternates were the same as those of voting jurors.

Trial I

Although the interviews were conducted by reference to a set of questions, jurors frequently shifted their responses to other subjects. For purposes of organization, the survey adheres generally to the sequence of a trial. There are several exceptions: the Miller Incident as the smoking gun will be treated separately, and because of readability and psycholinguistic studies, Part II will conclude with a discussion of instructions.

1. Market Share

Despite the argument over the relevant geographic market that ensued during deliberation, Jury I expressed very little concern or interest in this issue during interviews. CEI was big, and thus the actual dimensions of its size were irrelevant. They accepted the testimony of the city's economist, who ascribed a market to CEI of over 80 percent of sales. Moreover, the jurors did not relate CEI's size to the list of factors suggested by the court to be considered in determining the relevant geographic market.[52] What was most pronounced in the responses was Jury I's working backward from conduct to size; CEI engaged in bad conduct that hurt Muny, therefore CEI was exploiting its considerable size advantage.

2. CEI Conduct

In his opening statement, counsel for CEI posed the question: "Does General Motors have to help Chrysler?"[53] To CEI, the answer was obvious: in the world of competition, firms can't make money by helping rivals—especially less efficient rivals. It was therefore irrational and bad business for CEI to sell its power to Muny.

The majority of Jury I rejected this argument, instead adopting a public utility concept that generally favored competition in the distribution of electricity subject to a form of public interest responsibility. Maybe GM doesn't have to aid Chrysler, but CEI has a duty to cooperate with Muny to assure its reliability. As a juror observed, "Not charity—but they have an obligation."

This loosely defined version of a public utility's responsibility was a theme that threaded through interviews with the jurors (and alternates), and served as a basis for disapproval of CEI's refusal to interconnect and efforts to get Muny customers to switch. To Jury I, CEI's behavior had a negative effect on the community and, according to one juror, could not be justified: "No way CEI could go out of business, they can always go to [the Public Utilities Commission] and get more money." The foreman was explicit in her consumer orientation: "How would you feel if you were the one, the consumer, standing in between and have everybody say, well, we don't have the power to supply you, we are not going to sell it to them, so you guys are going to stay in the dark."

The jury fashioned their own version of a public interest responsibility to impose on the defendant. Undoubtedly, the testimony and arguments fertilized existing predilections that favored the city's David versus Goliath theme. A blue collar jury, Jury I viewed management wtih skepticism. They were suspicious of big business—which was synonymous with management. Muny, publicly owned and operated to provide power at low rates, was not deemed big business. Investor-owned CEI was big business since its sole objective was to make money.

The jury's strong association of Muny's interests with the interests of the community was a factor in their rejection of CEI's contention that Muny had a competitive edge due to tax exemptions. Tax advantages were translated into lower prices—a benefit to the community. The underlying belief was that if CEI had wanted to compete in prices it could have and still made a profit. As one juror stated, "CEI was too big and always made a profit." Another said, "I didn't feel sorry for 'poor old CEI'."[54]

3. Natural Monopoly

CEI's primary legal defense was that in the market in which Muny and CEI competed for the sale of retail electrical power, demand could be efficiently supplied by only one firm. Throughout the trial, defense counsel openly and persistently acknowledged that CEI aspired to be the sole survivor. With candor, he said, "We have admitted an intent to eliminate competition. If the elimination of competition...in a market such as this is unlawful under the Sherman Act, then we're in trouble."[55]

Having posed the natural monopoly defense in such blunt terms, successful implementation had to negotiate two obstacles: the concept had to be communicated to the jury so it could be understood and accepted as credible, and the jury had to be persuaded that it applied to the Muny-CEI struggle. Discussion with jurors and alternates on natural monopoly elicited three types of responses to the defense:

a. Comprehended the theory but it doesn't apply.
Only an alternate juror appeared to have understood the concept, although confessing that it was difficult. With a degree in engineering, this person was the best educated on the panel. Although vague in his description of the concept, he seemed to doubt both the credibility of the economic assumptions inherent in natural monopoly and its application to Cleveland—whatever the assumptions. His conclusion was that both utilities could have survived had not strong personalities and confrontation politics interfered. He apparently opted for the worst natural monopoly scenario—wasteful collusion rather than a fight to the finish.

b. Did not comprehend.
When the discussion moved from the facts of conduct to economic theory, the jurors became less confident and responsive. This was noticeable when natural monopoly was a topic, as *non sequitur* answers dominated. Everyone appeared to remember the term, that it involved competition, and that it was a CEI argument. Nevertheless, the thinness of their responses made it evident that they did not understand the concept sufficiently to apply it to the case. Although they were unable to explain the economic dynamics of natural monopoly, many jurors mentioned with approval the city's argument that the existence of two firms in the same market for over seventy years undercut the natural monopoly argument.

c. Natural monopoly was irrelevant to jurors who had already decided in favor of the city.
Any judgment on this point necessarily involves speculation. As will be discussed in Part III, studies show that jurors decide, albeit subconsciously, early during a trial and then look for evidence supporting or reinforcing their judgment. My surmise, for reasons discussed subsequently, is that this occurred to most of these jurors. The jurors certainly conveyed this impression in discussing natural monopoly. Several concluded that by its bad conduct, CEI had lost the right to raise this or any defense. One alternate stated that "CEI shouldn't have the attitude that this is a natural monopoly. A big company wanted to get everything." A juror noted in connection with natural monopoly: "Muny had a right to survive."

4. Damages, Proximate Cause, and Mismanagement
a. Calculation of Damages
Questions relating to damages generally elicited a soft response; jurors either shrugged their shoulders in disinterest or remarked, "We never got to it [in deliberation]." They had not retained the details of damage testimony. The one exception was an influential juror who allowed as how

the jury "would have been deliberating a long time, would have had to go back forty years." The most plausible explanation for the jury's lack of interest is that despite hearing extensive testimony on damages, they did not expect to be given the responsibility of calculation. As a group with virtually no jury experience, they sat through the trial assuming that their only function was to determine "guilt or innocence," without responsibility for calculating damages. Since the jury was extremely favorably inclined to the city's economic expert on damages, one can speculate that they would have awarded damages according to the city's demands.

b. Proximate Cause and Mismanagement

The final note I would like to make is that CEI will claim Muny Light mismanaged. There is no doubt about it that through the years from time to time Muny Light's manager made errors, but they did a pretty good job in the overall.[56]

—Plaintiff's opening statement

The second defense that we have is...mismanagement, and you will hear an incredible tale of mismanagement.[57]

—Defendant's opening statement

Although a principal factor in the trial, proximate cause did not become recognizable to the jury as a distinct legal issue until instructions and the receipt of special interrogatories. The jury lost or never acquired memory of the oral instructions' definition and hence initiated deliberations with reference to Interrogatory Three, which read: "[If you find CEI monopolized or attempted to monopolize] did CEI's conduct proximately cause damage to the business or property of the City of Cleveland?"[58]

Question Three, as the foreman observed, caused "a lot of trouble" and remained a problem until the court reread the instructions to the jury. Thereafter the jury's definition of proximate cause was reduced to the question: "Did CEI hurt Muny?" One juror, however, framed the issue as: "Did CEI cause some damage to Muny—even 2 percent?"

Proximate cause necessarily raises the issue of mismanagement. CEI sought to break the line of causation between conduct and injury by convincing the jury that Muny's wounds were self-inflicted. Jury I's dedication to a public interest doctrine led them to reject this argument. With the exception of the dissenter, the consensus was that Muny's problems were directly related to CEI's refusal to deal, not mismanagement. According to one juror, "Muny had their problems, but CEI wanted to make them worse." Several jurors pointed out that Muny had been in business since 1905. To one juror, the "competency of Muny was irrelevant."

The Miller Incident

The most publicized single event of the *Cleve. v. CEI* drama was the so-called Miller Incident, which involved a covert arrangement between two CEI officials and a Cleveland attorney to institute legal proceedings against Muny. Characterized by a Cleveland newspaper as "the most damaging testimony against CEI,"[59] the Miller Incident took on the notoriety of the classic smoking gun. Media interest in the event was fueled by the defense's strenuous efforts to have the matter excluded from the jury. Cleveland newspapers headlined the issue: "CEI Asks To Bar Tie-In Plot As Trial Evidence"[60] and "CEI's Secret Financing Of 1972 Suit Is An Issue In Antitrust Trial Today."[61]

1. CEI's Use of a Third Party

The parties stipulated that on March 8, 1972, the Federal Power Commission ordered the installation of a sixty-nine kilovolt emergency connection between CEI and Muny.[62] This was to be a nonsynchronous tie which would permit load transfers subject to interruption in customer service. On April 11, 1972, two CEI officials, the general counsel and the corporate solicitor, prepared a letter signed by the corporate solicitor and addressed to the city law director concerning the interconnection. According to the letter, "CEI will be happy to work with the City concerning the interconnection."[63] CEI followed this communication on May 12 by sending the city a right-of-way license agreement and "stating that the general route of the interconnection was approved."[64]

In the meantime, the two CEI officials conducted a series of meetings with Charles Miller, a Cleveland lawyer, to discuss a taxpayers' suit against the city. "During these conferences [the two CEI officials] gave Miller advice and technical information concerning the proposed taxpayer suit."[65] Miller filed the suit on May 9 in Cuyahoga County Common Pleas Court, seeking to enjoin the construction of the interconnection. The court allowed construction to continue but issued a six-day temporary restraining order that was subsequently dissolved and the complaint was dismissed on May 23.

The Miller Incident   37

Miller did not disclose CEI's participation in the lawsuit nor that he was compensated for his services and expenses by CEI.

2. Admissibility of the Miller Incident

According to the city, CEI's covert involvement in the Miller lawsuit constituted a form of monopolizing behavior because it demonstrated that the refusal to interconnect was part of a plan to "maintain and enhance" monopoly power.[66] Early in Trial I, Judge Krupansky rejected this argument, ruling that under the *Noerr*[67]-*Pennington*[68] doctrine, the "activity of soliciting others to institute lawsuits constitutes expressive conduct protected by the First Amendment."[69] He also rejected the plaintiff's contention that the Miller lawsuit was an abuse of the judicial process and therefore fell within the *sham* exception to the *Noerr-Pennington* rule. He stated:

> [T]he instant record as presently comprised, does not evidence a corruption or abuse of the judicial process within the purview of *California Motor Transport*.
>
> There is no suggestion, for example, that the litigation here in question entailed perjured testimony, the bribery of, or the conspiracy with, a public official, or any other aggravating circumstances akin to those enumerated and condemned in *California Motor Transport*.
>
> The fact that CEI covertly sponsored and financed the taxpayer suit would appear of little consequence. As the case authorities have recognized, that activity of soliciting others to institute lawsuits constitutes expressive conduct protected by the First Amendment.[70]

The court nevertheless left the door open by adding two qualifications. First, the stipulations could be admissible "for the limited purpose of showing 'the purpose and character of the particular transaction under scrutiny'... where the probative value of the proof outweighs the prejudicial impact."[71] Judge Krupansky concluded that the probative value of the stipulation had been diminished by CEI's express admission to the jury "that it fully intended to reduce or eliminate competition between it and Muny Light."[72]

Secondly, if CEI counsel elicited testimony from the witnesses that CEI had cooperated with the city in construction of the emergency interconnection, the Miller stipulation could be used for impeachment purposes.[73] This occurred during the first trial and the jury heard the judge read the stipulations on the last trial day. The stipulations were not allowed in evidence during Trial II.[74]

3. Effect on Jury I

The majority of Jury I rejected defense counsel's closing argument that the Miller Incident was of no consequence because it lasted only eleven days and did not, in fact, impede the installation of the emergency interconnection.[75] It is, however, doubtful that this evidence was the smoking gun that converted the majority to the city's cause. Instead, the survey reveals that while Miller made an impression, evidence of CEI's refusal to interconnect was the actual smoking gun. According to one juror, the Miller stipulation "carried some weight [and] was a piece in the puzzle." Another juror said that when he heard the stipulation, "I thought, what else has CEI done?" The foreman added that it was a factor in deliberation: "For us that was kind of like the real clincher."

My impression is that despite denials, many members of the jury followed the news media coverage of the trial. (It is interesting that some jurors claimed not to have looked at newspapers but accused other jurors of doing so.) As a result, members of Jury I were aware of the Miller Incident early in the trial, where it had the effect of contributing to the crystallization of negative views toward CEI.

Of relevance to the issue of comprehension of instructions (discussed below) is that the jury failed to grasp the limited purpose for which the stipulation was admitted to evidence. Although admitted for impeachment purposes only,[76] interviews indicate that many jurors assumed that it was to be considered and evaluated as a form of illegal conduct. Jurors described the use of Miller by CEI as a "cunning" act, a "dirty trick," and an example of CEI's effort to "put Muny out of business." One juror concluded that it was an illegal act in violation of the antitrust laws.

4. Trial II

One of the continuing dramas of Trial II was whether the Miller Incident would be presented to the jury. Newspaper articles publicized the drama with headlines such as: "Increasingly Vital CEI Document Is In Judge's Files."[77] CEI lawyers were walking a tightrope; if they elicited testimony from their witnesses that the court could construe as evidence that CEI cooperated in the installation of the sixty-nine kilovolt interconnection, the jury would hear about the Miller lawsuit. CEI lawyers successfully walked the tightrope and Jury II never heard the Miller stipulation. The newspaper headlines read: "CEI Avoids Damaging Evidence, Ends Defense."[78]

One can only speculate on Jury II's reaction if they had heard the stipulation. The jury's complete disdain for the city's case suggests that it would have had little, if any, effect. While one juror was equivocal on the Miller facts ("It may have [made a difference], it's hard to say"), several others indicated that it was an acceptable response in the competitive struggle between the plaintiff and the defendant. The foreman said, "If Muny had the right to force interconnection, why shouldn't CEI have the right to sue Muny?"

Deliberation: Trial I

Until the reading of the final oral instructions, Jury I had not been given any form of guidance or education as to how they were to discharge their responsibilities. They had virtually no jury experience and as a result several went through the trial assuming that their only function was to vote guilty or innocent. The law applicable to the case was orally communicated by Judge Krupansky in a one and a half hour lecture. Instructions included five special interrogatories, which for purposes of deliberation were the only written reference to the "law of the case."[79]

The accuracy of a re-creation of the deliberation by Jury I must take into account the deep bitterness that a 5-1 hung jury created. Thirteen days of unrelenting conflict had a traumatic effect; according to one news account describing the jurors after their discharge, "the panel left the courthouse a frustrated, bitter bunch."[80] Another newspaper described the scene as "an emotional explosion."[81]

There is some indication that seeds of tension, if not discontent, were sown with the election of the foreman. Several jurors had the impression that the dissenter aspired to be elected foreman, allegedly saying, "I'll take it if nobody else wants it." She lost the opportunity to the youngest juror (age twenty-six), who apparently was nominated because she occupied the first chair throughout the trial. "[S]he [the holdout] didn't seem too well pleased when the rest of us asked C. to be [foreman] because she was sitting in the number one seat and that was the reason we asked, not because we thought she knew more than anyone else...."

The foreman sought to impose an authoritarian ("structured and organized")[82] procedure on the deliberation. She initiated the discussion by reading to the group the first special interrogatory on the relevant geographic market and then circulated the question form for individual scrutiny. Each juror was then requested to render an opinion in the exact sequence the question form was circulated. The foreman was, in effect, conducting a straw vote.

Research indicates that conducting a straw vote at the initial stages of deliberation can undermine efficient problem solving.[83] Complex legal and factual issues create high levels of anxiety among jurors. Tension levels are exacerbated by the admonition not to discuss the case while it is in progress. One method of reducing anxiety is through a straw vote; it is a quick way to get answers on the table. It also may have negative consequences:

> This is undesirable juror conduct because each individual is placed in a position of making a commitment to the other jurors. Right or wrong, each juror will probably feel inclined to defend his "position" throughout the deliberations. Such a commitment so early in the jury's vital work prevents full, rational consideration of the issues and evidence of the case.[84]

The effort to impose a systematic discussion procedure triggered immediate confrontation between foreman and dissenter. The foreman complained that the dissenter refused to adhere to the procedure by interrupting others. As a consequence, deliberations were started with argument and friction:

> So a lot of time [a juror] would start talking because [he] sat next to me and he would have been the first one to give his opinion and boy, he would start talking and the [dissenter] would start talking, and they were both talking and they got in more arguments.

The holdout had a different perspective:

> We passed the question around... then they decided to vote.... [N]o review of evidence, no review of anything. After the questionnaire we passed around... then we're gonna vote. I said no, we couldn't do that.

The discord over procedure fertilized confusion and disagreement over the first special interrogatory dealing with the relevant geographic market. The initial problem was comprehension, which was ostensibly "solved" when a juror purchased a pocket dictionary during a lunch break so the jury could get a definition of *relevant*. The discussion then settled into sharp disagreement over the boundaries of the relevant geographic market; the dissenter advocated a market comprised of thirty square miles of direct competition between Muny and CEI, while the majority argued for a Cleveland-plus market. According to the dissenter, if Muny was having problems serving its own customers, it could not expand into further competition with CEI. By the end of the second full day of deliberation, the jury unanimously agreed to the Cleveland-plus market, a consensus that was broken the next morning when the dissenter changed her mind.

This exacerbated the quickly developing disharmony and sparked a new crisis: Does a juror have the right to change an answer to an interrogatory? The foreman sought to assure finality by having each juror sign the interrogatory form as an acknowledgment that the answer to that question could not be rescinded. The dissenter signed the first interrogatory, accepting the Cleveland-plus market "for the sake of progress after such . . . arguing and debating. . . ." The jury went on to the second interrogatory dealing with monopolization and attempt to monopolize.

Already in conflict, the disagreement between majority and dissenter widened and hardened on the monopolization issue. The bulk of the majority's argument was carried on by the foreman and another juror, who endeavored to persuade the dissenter that CEI had engaged in "underhanded" and "sleazy" conduct. The dissenter stood firm on the argument that CEI was entitled to compete as aggressively as Muny and that a public utility like CEI had no more responsibility to aid a rival than any other private enterprise. Disagreement on CEI's refusal to interconnect set the tone for the remainder of the deliberation. The foreman summarized her perceptions of the disagreement:

> She didn't think that they [CEI] had to help. That's when we really got hung up in digging through [the exhibits], that's about one of the first days that we really spent all day. Nobody talked for like almost three hours that one morning. . . . We were digging up and just writing stuff down on paper, everybody was just busy reading and it was funny because we were looking for anything that we could prove to her that it [CEI's conduct] was more or less underhanded or dirty. . . ."

The dissenter thought that the third special interrogatory, dealing with proximate cause, was the real problem. To her, mismanagement was the proximate cause of Muny's failure—a view not shared by the majority. Other jurors agreed that it was indeed a problem, but to them the problem was in understanding the meaning of the term. Agreeing that the dictionary was of no help, the jury turned to the judge, who reread the instructions to them. This satisfied the majority, who henceforth defined proximate cause as, "Did CEI harm Muny?" The dissenter disagreed with that interpretation because it failed to take into consideration Muny's mismanagement.

The dissenter conceded that CEI had done the acts alleged in the city's testimony—but refused to sign Interrogatory Three because CEI "had a reason" to engage in such behavior. She would have signed her assent to the question if she could have also written down the reasons justifying CEI's actions. The foreman refused, stating that those reasons would be relevant to damages.

The dissenter refused to capitulate and after thirteen days of turmoil and disagreement, Judge Krupansky declared a mistrial. It was a classic, hard-nosed hung jury struggle between two strong-willed individuals. The dissenter charged that she was accused of being dumb, and that the foreman threatened to have her removed from the jury unless she went along with the majority. This, plus other harassment, made the dissenter "angry enough to knock the hell out of her [the foreman]." Conversely, the majority viewed the holdout as a troublemaker, resentful for not being elected foreman, and unreasonably biased in favor of CEI.[85]

A newspaper described the jury room after the dismissal of the jury:

> On the bulletin board was a doodle, a scrap of paper that crudely depicted these six angry people. An alternate drew it during the trial to parody a newspaper-type sketch. The doodle was found; so was a dictionary. A bookmark was tucked inside the paperback volume on page 513. The page included the definition of "monopoly." It included the definition of "monstrosity," too.[86]

Trial II

1. The Interim

During the nearly eight month interim between Trials I and II, *Cleve. v. CEI* was a frequent media topic. Whether the city should use its 5-1 favorable jury vote as leverage and seek settlement was debated in the newspapers.[87] A newspaper poll showed that 82 percent favored a retrial.[88] The mayor, council president, and council debated the availability of funds to finance a second trial.[89] A former mayor threatened to start an initiative petition drive to force a retrial.[90] CEI's president kept media attention on the case by announcing that any damages would be passed on to the public, a statement that triggered negative editorial commentary.[91]

Media attention also focused on the legal maneuvers. Citing the "inflammatory content of the daily publicity" given Trial I, CEI requested that the second trial be shifted to Cincinnati.[92] Subsequently, the city and CEI agreed to a delay in order to permit the city's expert economist to have open heart surgery.[93]

2. Trial II and the Déjà Vu Factor

We will present basically the same case we did in the first trial. The facts haven't changed. We were confident during the first trial and we are confident.[94]

—City's lead counsel

I'm not going to answer any questions.[95]

—CEI's lead counsel

There is debate over the effects of a mistrial. It has been suggested that the tactical and psychological edge shifts to the defendant. According to this argument, the defense exploits the opportunity to "learn in the first trial how you put your case together, the tack you take, and which points are primary points and which are giveaways."[96] This assumes that the plaintiff has presented its best case and hence will not engage in drastic revision.

This is an assumption that the defendant could rationally make. While some tinkering could be expected, it would have been difficult to justify rewriting a script that appealed to five of six jurors (and most of the alternates). Not only did the defense have a roadmap of the city's case and profiles on the witnesses' personalities, but they had an opportunity to observe their opponents' advocacy styles. Moreover, with a single vote preventing defeat, the defense *had* to revise strategy and be more "creative" and "self-critical."[97]

3. Advocacy Tactics

The CEI defense team made two changes in advocacy tactics. They increased the frequency of technical objections on evidentiary points, with particular emphasis on the failure to lay a proper foundation and on improper leading questions. In addition, lead counsel increased the intensity and vigor of his cross-examination of key city witnesses.

a. Objection

There is a risk that frequent objections will alienate the jury.[98] The concern is that the jury will become irritated with the interruption in the flow of testimony and/or will form the impression that the objector is creating a smoke screen for a weak case. CEI adhered to the textbook convention during Trial I by raising few objections on technical evidentiary grounds. Now aware that the city followed a set script of questions, CEI changed tactics by increasing the tempo of objections. According to one of the defense lawyers:

> And, that's the reason we changed in the second trial. We thought they operated from essentially a set piece. They had prepared....
>
> QUESTION: A script you mean.
>
> ANSWER: Right. They had prepared exhaustively. You could literally tell that they were reading the questions almost in their entirety. And they were getting back answers that had been probably rehearsed with the witness beforehand. That's not uncommon and I'm not being critical of it but that's the way they did it. When somebody does it that way, it seems to me you can discombobulate them a little bit by being technical and throwing them off.
>
> QUESTION: So, that's part of your change in strategy.
>
> ANSWER: Sure, oh yes, definitely. To object more, to be more technical. We thought they weren't quite as adept at changing the script, so to speak, on the spot. As well they otherwise might have been. And, therefore, we decided if we objected we could throw off the presentation. And, I think it worked.[99]

The defense's new strategy was also a response to a jury poll indicating that the jurors held a high opinion of the advocacy skills of the city's lawyers. The assumption was that this impression could be prevented from surfacing in Trial II by use of aggressive tactics which would expose what the defense perceived as inexperience on the part of city lawyers.

Throughout Trial II, the court gave the defense favorable rulings on its objections. Interviews reveal that the jury was favorably impressed with the defendant's success. On occasion, the jurors heard rulings and comments made at bench conferences. The cumulative effect was the formation of a negative impression of the city lawyers' advocacy skills and the credibility of the case. (This will be discussed in greater depth in "The Court's Influence on the Jury," Part III, *infra*.)

There was also a dramatic difference between Trials I and II in the number of objections. In Trial I, during the direct testimony of W.H., a key witness for the city, the defense objected a total of seventeen times; eleven were sustained, five overruled, and one withdrawn. At one point, the court advised a passive defense counsel that "technically an objection would lay,"[100] an invitation which was ignored.

When W.H.'s direct examination by the city began in midafternoon of July 21, 1981, the new Trial II strategy was initiated. The explosion occurred on the next day with a barrage of forty-three objections, twenty-nine of which were sustained. Sometimes complaining of repetitious testimony, defense most frequently objected to leading questions. The mood was volatile, with the defense complaining:

> He's your witness, surely you know what he's going to say. But for you to go on question after question like you were on cross-examination, I find it offensive, and it's objectionable, and it required me to get up in front of the jury and appear to be making petty objections from time to time, and I resent being put in that position by somebody who ought to know better.[101]

Direct examination was completed in the early afternoon of the following day, when sixteen objections were made. Tempers over the leading question dispute reached a crescendo during a morning break when, according to a Cleveland newspaper, "shouting turned to shoving"[102] between opposing lead counsel.

In contrast to the defense's tactics, plaintiff objected only forty-five times during the nearly five days of W.H.'s cross-examination. They were sustained fourteen times and overruled thirty-one times. The cross-examination was characterized by evident animosity between the witness and defense counsel. The tension was increased by the court's frequent reprimands of the witness for not responding to the question.

b. *Cross-examination*

A strong interrogator during Trial I, defense lead counsel increased the length and energy of cross-examination in the second trial. It was a risky tactic, since Jury I had formed a negative opinion of his performance, accusing him of being unnecessarily "hard," "belligerent," and "intolerant" of the city's witnesses.

Again the defense used the experience of Trial I to an advantage. Carefully reading the transcripts, counsel prepared a cross-examination book. "Each subject was tabbed and we had outlines and indexes for all the different documents and things said on direct and the inconsistent things said...."[103] The defense earmarked two of the city's important witnesses, W.H. and Dr. W., for special attention.

(i) W.H.

As commissioner of light and power during parts of 1971-73, W.H. was an important source of knowledge for plaintiff. Hired by the Stokes administration to rehabilitate Muny and a strong advocate of publicly owned electrical power systems, W.H. participated in the interconnection negotiations with CEI, and had engaged in other activities relevant to the city's allegations. According to a Cleveland newspaper, "H., an electrical engineer, accountant and adamant proponent of public power, took on CEI and spearheaded City attempts to get a permanent electrical hookup with CEI and to get the Company to relay cheap out-of-state power to Muny Light."[104]

W.H. made a relatively brief appearance in the first trial. His direct examination consumed a little over one and a half days and 258 pages of transcript. The cross-examination was completed in around one day (165 transcript pages), with four questions on redirect and one on recross.

W.H.'s cross-examination was interrupted several times for the testimony of other city witnesses. According to a CEI lawyer, this provided the defense with an additional benefit: "By putting other people on, all they did was to give us more time to go back through H.'s direct and pick out things we wanted to cross-examine him about."[105]

In Trial II, the defense vigorously attacked W.H. The direct examination took slightly over two days while the cross-examination lasted approximately five days. Direct examination made up 334 transcript pages, 678 for cross-examination, 112 pages for redirect and 69 pages for recross.

W.H. was an influential witness in both trials. His testimony persuaded Jury I that Muny's success depended on the permanent interconnection, that CEI resorted to delaying ploys, and that Muny's demise came from CEI's actions, not mismanagement. His testimony was described as "significant" and "covered everything." He "exposed" CEI and his testimony was remembered in deliberation when it was used to rebut the dissenter.

In Trial II, W.H.'s testimony was pivotal. The consensus among Jury

II was that aggressive and pugnacious cross-examination flushed out damaging remarks that seriously, if not fatally, undermined the city's case. The jury was highly critical of everything associated with W.H.'s testimony. For example, his varied employment background, introduced to demonstrate his qualifications as an expert, was seen as evidence of unreliability: "He can't keep a job." They were shocked when he acknowledged being paid fifty dollars per hour for his services to the city. The jury assumed that his evasion on cross-examination was a ploy to increase his paycheck. The foreman observed, "When he came up to get his cross-examination, he avoided everything. We couldn't figure out if he was getting paid by the hour or the sentence." As the chief architect of Muny's revival, W.H.'s failure to cope with the blistering cross-examination furnished a strong boost to CEI's mismanagement argument. As a juror observed, "after they were through with him [on cross-examination], I could see why Muny went downhill."

(ii) Dr. W.

Dr. W., the city's economics expert, testified longer than any other witness. He had the responsibility for explaining the antitrust and economics rationale of the city's case by presenting testimony on concepts such as market power, relevant geographic market, anticompetitive behavior, natural monopoly, and damages.

Dr. W. was a formidable witness; his personal convictions were with the city's case, he was a knowledgeable and experienced witness, and he appeared to enjoy verbal combat with the defense. During Trial I, his energy level was, however, drained by a heart condition, which was corrected before Trial II.

During Trial I, Dr. W. testified on three separate occasions: on competition, October 7–9; on damages, October 14–15; and in rebuttal, October 28. He spent a total of approximately four days on the stand, with his testimony consuming 633 transcript pages. During plaintiff's direct and redirect questioning, defense counsel's objections were sustained forty-one times and overruled nine times. On defendant's cross and recross, plaintiff's counsel was never sustained and was overruled ten times.

The most frequent objection by defense charged Dr. W. with nonresponsive answers. As the testimony continued, the court became critical of the witness and the lawyers.[106]

To Jury I, Dr. W. was the most persuasive and effective witness to testify. Several jurors indicated that they had better recall of his testimony than any other witness. They approved of his willingness to answer any question, felt that he didn't evade, was "candid" and "stuck to his guns." The foreman was particularly impressed with Dr. W.'s performance, even attending a session of Trial II for a repeat performance.

Dr. W. was the catalyst that channeled the perceptions of Jury I. He impressed the jurors with his academic background and experience, which "made him more credible than all of CEI's witnesses." His testimony gave a ring of credibility to previous witnesses. His skirmishes on cross-examination enhanced the image of the little guy battling the aggressive predator that the city was endeavoring to foster.

As a result of successful open heart surgery between trials, Dr. W. was healthier—and more pugnacious—in Trial II. During her visit to the second trial, the Jury I foreman got this response when she complimented him on his improved physical appearance: "He said, 'Yeah, I'm feeling a lot stronger now, I might even get them this time.' You know," continued the foreman, "he was really...out there to get them." The press summed up Dr. W.'s Trial II energetic demeanor: "W. repeatedly challenged questions, suggesting they were not questions but statements, were double statements or were simplistic."[107]

Statistics confirm the elevation of hostilities between CEI's counsel and Dr. W. Almost doubling the statistics of Trial I, Dr. W. spent a total of around seven days testifying, consuming 1,143 pages of the transcript. Overall, defense's objections were sustained forty-three times, overruled nineteen times.

Dr. W.'s testimony was rejected by Jury II. To them, his credibility was destroyed by a needlessly aggressive style that was manifest in evasive and argumentative answers. The foreman observed:

> [H]e did have a tendency that when there was a question that he could answer yes or no, he never did. It was always, "yes," then he would give a 15 minute dissertation. To me, it was insulting my intelligence.

Another juror accused the witness of talking down to them:

> [I] don't think he wants you to understand him.... [W]ell, he is a teacher and he is used to lecturing and we are not his students. He was very proud of his papers...I thought he was up there on an ego trip most of the time.

On numerous occasions the court complained of Dr. W.'s unresponsiveness and his verbal evasions. To the court, the witness was deliberately ignoring instructions and rulings. On August 24, 1981, Judge Krupansky expressed his frustration to the lawyers:

> THE COURT: What are we going to do with friend W.?
>
> MS. C.: I hope we will finish his direct today, Your Honor.
>
> THE COURT: Well, over the weekend, I have gone over his testimony and I don't know how much more of his testimony this record can take because he's departed into areas that have been ruled out of this case on a number of occasions.
>
> First of all, on two occasions, the antitrust case before the NRC—CEI's

Trial II

antitrust case before the NRC—CAPCO cases before the NRC, and he got into this area of price influence.

Then he got into just conjecture, special referendum, which has been ruled out; and now he's in this area of effective regulation, which I have directly ruled out.

In reading his testimony over the weekend, the entire thrust of his testimony is that there is no effective regulation by the PUCO.

I just can't handle this fellow. I have instructed him on a number of occasions. I'm sure that you have instructed him Ms. C.; as I say, I have had an examination of the law made, and I suppose I could completely exclude his testimony, which I am not desirous of doing.

I could cite him for contempt or failure to conform to the Court's orders, which I'm not desirous of doing.

The only effective way that I can handle the matter is to *voir dire* him and edit the testimony and read it to the jury. That way, the City can place before the jury the material evidence which it is permitted to place before the jury, we avoid all of the highly prejudicial inflammatory areas which have been the pitfalls of his testimony, and these obfuscations that he gets into.

I mean, he just makes statements that are untrue.[108]

On October 6, during cross-examination of Dr. W.'s rebuttal, Judge Krupansky made good his threat to *voir dire* the witness. Since the jurors had already formed a negative impression of Dr. W., *voir dire* made no impression on them. Indeed, most jurors felt that Dr. W. was the beneficiary because "we didn't hear what an ass he would have made of himself by further testimony...."

4. Substantive Changes: Mismanagement

In Trial I, the defense used mismanagement to interrupt the line of proximate cause from CEI conduct to Muny's demise. Defense counsel changed strategy to "broaden the scope of [mismanagement] to a defense to the entire case on the merits."[109] It was an effective move that fatally infected the city's monopolization argument.

Early in Trial II the plaintiff created the opening for the mismanagement theme by presenting testimony on Muny's finances and operational capability. Exploiting this opportunity,[110] CEI's cross-examination elicited a range of commentary: a consulting engineer's recommendation to replace a 1914 generator;[111] "downward trend [of Muny] was toward...economic disaster";[112] "plant was in need of rehabilitation";[113] "using these archaic old generators";[114] "Muny Light has more employees per customer [than CEI]";[115] "CEI's cost [per kilowatt hour] was $3.59...and Muny Light's was $6.49";[116] "severe outages in the Municipal Electric Light Plant which then caused the Mayor to request the Director to meet with CEI officials";[117]

"when the Municipal services were so very poor";[118] "massive [Muny] outages which required direct action."[119]

These early references to a history of operational problems surprised the jurors and created doubt in their minds as to the credibility of the city's case. According to the foreman:

> I thought that the city was on trial, because they were...trying to justify their management boo-boos. And, I am saying, wait a minute, in my mind I'm saying, what are they doing...here, we're supposed to be proving that CEI did something against them and all they are talking about is how they built their plant...and the things that went wrong with it.

Politics was introduced as the source of mismanagement. To Jury II, Muny was a political enterprise, incompetently run by bureaucrats. "I don't know," one juror queried, "how politicians know about management and about running a business. They were too busy. They don't know what they are doing."

The jury assumed that as political appointees and therefore lacking job security, Muny managers lacked the motivation to excel. Moreover, the fact that wages were not competitive resulted in the best talent getting experience and then crossing over to the investor-owned utilities. The result, according to the foreman, was that "you are not going to get quality people in there that are ever going to care." The jury drew a contrast with CEI executives, who testified to long careers of working up through the ranks.

The politics and mismanagement theme dominated the trial. The jury attributed Muny's power outages and general unreliability to incompetent management. Likewise, they saw Muny's fiscal crisis as a function of political infighting rather than CEI's conduct. Defense counsel's exposure of cross-subsidization with other city operations made an impression. In evaluating the city's demand for permanent interconnection, the foreman said: "CEI has to be right in saying that...we will give you an interconnection to bring your rates up, you start making money so you won't have to live off the city...like they took the money from the...Water or Sewer Department."

Jury II's strong feelings against political involvement in business is best dramatized by their hostile reaction to the mayor of Cleveland's testimony. When asked where the city would get funds for rehabilitating Muny, the mayor said, "In this case, I hope you pay for it when we win the lawsuit."[120] The mildest comment was that the mayor made a "boo-boo." Most members of Jury II were incensed and felt that his appearance was a political ploy to influence them. In the succinct words of a juror: "He was cocky...he just made a fool of himself."

5. Market Power: Relevant Geographic Market

The jury's perception of Muny as wrecked by mismanagement and in deep fiscal crisis was a significant factor in resolution of the relevant geographic market. The defendant argued that the thirty square mile area where the utilities directly competed was the relevant market. The city suggested the city of Cleveland, plus a small area leading to a sewage plant. The issue was critical: in the city's version of the relevant market, CEI controlled over 80 percent of retail power sales (which is presumptive of monopoly power), while in CEI's proposed market, CEI controlled only 57 percent of sales. Jury II chose the thirty square mile area; the foreman summarized:

> But then, like I said, going back to the Sherman Act and its stating that it's the area that there is direct competition. In other words, that's the area where everybody has their machinery, or whatever, like in this case the lines and the poles are there now. This is the area that you restrict as the relevant market. There was...in that Sherman Act, said...the "potential." I said, well, we're not going with the potential because we're in 1975, '71 to '75, the city is broke, Muny is broke so there is no room for them to expand. So, we can't go and look at the whole city of Cleveland. And, then we finally broke it down between the evidence and the Sherman Act as it's right where they are now, competing.

The relevant market issue was not, however, dispositive to the jury's decision. When asked to assume a CEI market share of 80 percent plus, their reactions continued to focus on two points: Muny was mismanaged, therefore CEI's size was irrelevant, and CEI's conduct was a legitimate expression of competition.

6. Conduct

Unlike Jury I, Jury II did not assign a public interest responsibility to CEI but instead viewed the confrontation as normal competition. Conceding that CEI had engaged in activities designed to inhibit, if not terminate, Muny, the collective attitude of the jury was, "So what?" Aggressive efforts to get new business is rational competition. One juror compared the free wiring customer strategy to her husband's giving special inducements to his customers. "They were offering something and I don't see anything wrong with it." To the foreman, free wiring was "investing money" to increase rates and thereby "make money."

It was evident that the jury was influenced by the perception of a mismanaged Muny seeking to use an efficiently operated CEI as a convenient crutch for rehabilitation.

7. Natural Monopoly

CEI embellished and reorganized its natural monopoly package with new witnesses. A new witness introduced the theoretical underpinnings of the concept, followed by another new witness who described his empirical survey of decreasing duplication of competing utilities in the United States. The remaining witnesses testified to Cleveland's characteristics as a natural monopoly.[121]

Jurors either openly acknowledged complete lack of understanding of the concept or gave rambling interpretations that revealed no comprehension.[122] Here is an example of the latter:

> Well, I think they did [explain natural monopoly], because it is my understanding of a natural monopoly is when you are a very strong company, you've got whatever it takes, money, power, to become a monopoly to knock your competition out of business, and the thing there is I guess he was saying maybe it was illegally done.

To the foreman, natural monopoly was a consequence of mismanagement; the demise of Muny through mismanagement would leave CEI with a natural monopoly. Another juror assumed that a natural monopoly was the consequence of natural forces, and CEI was simply "building their company in a natural way."

8. Damages—Proximate Cause

There was general agreement that it would have been difficult, if not impossible, to calculate damages. The jurors were in awe of the complexity of the task and conceded their inadequacy: "I think I would have floundered on that one"; "I don't know how you come up with the amounts—I really don't know." One of the alternate jurors assumed that the judge would determine damages.

To the foreman and other jurors, the conclusion that mismanagement severed the proximate cause link between CEI's conduct and injury rendered damages a moot issue. According to the foreman:

> How could you claim damages when you haven't made money for the last 15 years?... I said how could you claim $35 million damages when you guys haven't made a million dollars a year? You could assume you could make it, but first you have to make it one time before you could assume you would have made it.

9. Deliberation

> We didn't know one thing because the girl upstairs told us that normally they give out books telling jurors what is expected of them. But she said Judge Krupansky did not want that. So we just went with what he told us to do and that was it.
>
> —Juror, Trial II

Trial II

Like Jury I, Jury II had no predeliberation knowledge of their responsibilities. They did not anticipate the special interrogatories and, like Jury I, several assumed that a guilty or innocent verdict would discharge their duties. Unlike the first trial, however, the judge allowed the jury to take one copy of the instructions into deliberation.

The election of the foreman was conducted quickly and without tension as the occupant of the first chair was elected. The foreman was the most expressive and animated person and was an extremely skillful dominant juror. In managing the deliberation, his style was participatory rather than authoritarian, and he convened the jury as a committee.

Temporarily ignoring the interrogatories, the foreman began deliberations with an open-ended discussion by asking each juror to give her general impression of the case. His objective was to "get an idea where we stand." He advised his colleagues, "once we know where we are at, then we can start going through what he [Judge Krupansky] gave us...."

From the beginning of the deliberation, four jurors, including the foreman, expressed strong, if not conclusive, reservations about the city's case, while two jurors were "questionable." After this was established through the preliminary discussion, attention was then directed to the first interrogatory on the relevant geographic market. Without reaching a decision, the jury then went on to discuss the second question on monopolization, and then returned to Question One.

Since a broke and badly mismanaged Muny had neither the resources nor the inclination to expand beyond existing boundaries, the jury selected the thirty square mile area of direct competition as the relevant market. Within this market, CEI sold around 57 percent of retail electricity.

Several jurors indicated that resolution of the first interrogatory was irrelevant, since the basic issue was the legality of CEI's conduct. As noted earlier, the foreman revealed that even if CEI had controlled 80 percent of the market, his decision would have been the same.

The soft committee style employed by the foreman effectively accommodated the concerns of the two cautious jurors:

> I said, so now the best thing to do is let's take it step by step. You tell me what you find wrong and then we will dig up the evidence and prove it and, like I said, because we had the four people [who] were 100 percent in agreement and the two were questionable. I said, there's no way I want to go back into that courtroom and you have in your mind that you made the wrong decision.... So they would throw their questions out and each person would answer them, and if they felt there was some evidence they would dig it out.

Any trace of doubt in the two jurors was erased through a discussion of the instructions on credibility of witnesses, preponderance of the evidence, and purpose of the Sherman Act. They concluded that the city's witnesses were evasive, misleading, and unconvincing. Moreover, the Sherman Act espouses competition and CEI's conduct was a competitive reaction to Muny's efforts to get more customers. In light of this interpretation of the evidence, the city failed to prove its complaint by a preponderance of the evidence.

Instructions

1. Introduction

Federal district courts are required to instruct juries on the applicable law.[123] Courts have wide discretion in the phrasing of instructions and have the option of defining issues and allegations, describing rules for evaluating evidence and commenting on evidence and witnesses.[124] As Judge Krupansky instructed Juries I and II, under the accepted division of labor, "the jury decides the disputed facts and the court provides the instructions of law."[125]

The present status of instructions is the result of early tensions between judge and jury. Because of the colonial antagonism toward the judiciary, juries retained the right to resolve both questions of fact and law. Under these conditions, instructions were superfluous and judges "frequently gave no instructions at all, relying on the jurors to be 'good judges of the common law of the land'."[126] The modern division of labor was introduced in 1895, when the Supreme Court rejected the right of federal juries to decide the law.[127] One significant consequence was that once the trial court assumed the responsibility for providing the rules of law, the appellate courts were given the power to review instructions for errors of law.

Intimidation by the review process and fear of reversal created pressures on trial courts that, in turn, lead to a communication gap between judge and jury. According to a federal district judge:

> As trial instructions became subject to potentially demanding appellate review they became prolix, inconsistent, and excessively technical. Trial judges, uncertain of what might be required by the appellate courts, adopted lengthier and more complex instructions in the hope that they would leave few grounds upon which to base a reversal.[128]

Complex litigation, especially antitrust cases, adds more static in the communication channel between instruction and jury. Lengthy trials, complex facts, and vague laws must be distilled into instructions comprehensible to a jury of laymen.

2. A Precis of the Instructions

It took Judge Krupansky approximately two hours and ten minutes to read the final instructions to Jury I. At the beginning of Trial II, the court read preliminary instructions to the jury, describing in general terms the "words, phrases, and terminology which will be used by the lawyers and witnesses during the course of the trial."[129] The court also briefly described the alleged violations and relevant legal principles. The reading of final instructions to Jury II also took around two hours and ten minutes.[130]

Hence, after months of testimony, the jury received a two-hour crash course in antitrust. The challenge of comprehending the arcane rules of antitrust is revealed in a brief overview description of the final instructions on the city's basic claim: monopolization.

a. Monopolization

Using the accepted definition, the court instructed the jury that monopolization requires proof of market power and the acquisition or willful maintenance of that power.

Market power is "the power to control prices or exclude competition"[131] within a relevant market. The jury learned that a relevant market is composed of product and geographic components. Determination of the relevant geographic market requires "a pragmatic" judgment as to where the "sellers involved effectively compete and to which the purchasers involved can effectively turn as a source of supply."[132] As a matter of law, Judge Krupansky held retail electric power to be the relevant product market.

In determining whether CEI possessed power to control prices, the jury was instructed to take into consideration the Public Utility Commission's power to mandate prices charged by CEI, and to assume as a matter of law that the Public Utility Commission's authority to regulate rates "was properly and effectively exercised."[133] The jury was further advised that while normally a predominant market share was indicative of market power, this assumption "may not apply in a case involving a regulated defendant such as CEI."[134]

To prove the "willful acquisition or maintenance of market power," the city had to convince the jury that CEI had engaged in "exclusionary or restrictive" behavior which the court defined as conduct which "actually excludes actual or potential competition...and is unreasonable or unnecessary to competition on the merits."[135]

The city alleged that CEI's refusal to permanently interconnect constituted willful maintenance of market power, since it blocked Muny's purchase of CEI and PASNY power. The jury was told that Sherman section 2 prohibits refusals to deal in cases where the defendant possesses market power and the refusal is, "under the particular circumstances...unreasonably anticompetitive."[136] To determine whether the refusal is "unreasonably anticompetitive," the jury must consider three factors: (1) "market impact"; (2) the "fairness and efficiency" of the act; and (3) the existence of "valid business reasons."[137]

b. Refusal to Deal

Judge Krupansky identified the essential facility doctrine as a distinct type of refusal to deal. Control of an essential facility, such as CEI's transmission lines, "may impose...the duty to permit others fair and reasonable access thereto."[138] For CEI's transmission lines to constitute an essential facility, the jury must find that duplication of the lines would be "economically infeasible" and that "denial of its use would inflict a severe competitive handicap"[139] on Muny.

To satisfy these requirements, the city had to prove that it was not reasonably feasible for Muny to construct transmission lines, and that the denial of access to CEI facilities "severely impacted upon plaintiff's ability to compete."[140] Assuming an affirmative finding on these points, the jury must then balance three factors: (1) whether CEI wheeled power to others "similarly situated" to Muny; (2) the existence of "valid business reasons" for denial of access; and (3) "significant consideration of fairness or efficiency" justifying CEI's conduct.[141]

c. Natural Monopoly

After instructing on attempt to monopolize and proximate cause, the court described the affirmative defense of natural monopoly. Judge Krupansky gave the jury this definition:

> [A] monopoly resulting from economies of scale, a relationship between the size of the market and the size of the most efficient firm such that one firm of efficient size can produce all or more than the market can take at a remunerative price, and can continually expand its capacity at less cost than that of a new firm entering the business.[142]

In a natural monopoly, the intention to be the sole survivor or the successful achievement of that goal does not necessarily violate the Sherman Act. To prove a violation, there must be evidence that the defendant "foresees a fight to the finish [and] intends or actually does use unfair or predatory tactics."[143]

Acknowledging that *predatory* and *unfair* have "no well-defined meanings," Judge Krupansky told the jury to ascertain whether CEI endeavored to prevail in the natural monopoly "regardless of competitive merits on the basis of artificial restraints on the competitive process, which restraints not only have a significant effect to eliminate competitors unfairly, but which also confer no net benefits of superior efficiency on the public in the process."[144]

According to the court, CEI's customer strategy of providing free wiring could constitute predation if the defendant sacrificed present revenues to drive Muny from the market and then recouped its losses. It would not be predation, however, if the customer strategy was "fairly and reasonably designed to meet a lower price already being charged by a competitor."[145] Judge Krupansky's concluding instructions on damages included consideration of possible future losses, consideration of inflation, and a discount formula.

3. The Jury Gets the Instructions

The utility of instructions to a jury is a function of several factors. If the instructions were oral only, did the jury understand the information sought to be imported, and did they remember in sufficient detail to achieve effective recall during deliberation? Written instructions made available to the jury eliminates the memory factor, thereby isolating comprehension as the critical problem. Since comprehension is likely to vary among jurors, this creates the possibility that education efforts may be undertaken: knowledgeable jurors explain complicated material to other jurors. Education may fail, with jurors gravitating to portions they understand. Another possibility is that regardless of comprehension, jurors may rely on selected portions to rationalize a predetermined decision.

a. Jury I

After thirty trial days extending over eight weeks, Jury I received final instructions on November 10, 1981. Speaking in a soft but clear monotone, Judge Krupansky began reading from a manuscript at around 10:20 a.m., gave the jury a five to ten minute break an hour later, and concluded at approximately 12:40 p.m. This was the jury's first and last exposure to the legal principles they were to apply to the information received over the course of the trial.

What effect did the instructions have on the jury's decision-making process, and did they comprehend the legal standards they were to apply? With the exception of the dissenter, who described the instructions as "clear enough," the jurors candidly acknowledged that they did not—or had difficulty—understanding the charge. Instructions were "too long," "too complicated," and "too broad." The most educated juror, an alternate with a degree in engineering, concluded that they were "too long and hard to follow." The following colloquy with the foreman reveals the ineffectiveness of the charge:

> QUESTION: So when you went in the juryroom all you had to go by were

the questions [special interrogatories], and the instructions were of no help to you at all?

ANSWER: No, because we couldn't remember what he said. That's terrible but when you are getting nervous toward the end you really, we paid attention as much as we could but we couldn't remember what he said and the only instructions we could remember over and over again was don't discuss the case and don't read the newspapers and all that, you know, don't discuss the case with anybody.

The bottom line is that Jury I decided the fate of a $49 (trebled to almost $150) million lawsuit without remembering the final instructions. In deliberation, attention focused on the five special interrogatories, which in turn caused problems in comprehension. As noted earlier, a juror purchased a pocket dictionary to look up *relevant* (market) and *monopoly*. The third interrogatory on proximate cause so frustrated the jury that they requested, and received, a rereading of the instructions on that point. Interviews indicate that they never fully understood the meaning of the term. (*See* "Trial I: Proximate Cause and Mismanagement," *supra*.) Instructions on the Miller Incident, the so-called smoking gun, were misconstrued or ignored. Admitted for impeachment purposes, it was deemed monopolizing conduct.

Despite expressions of frustration with the instructions and acknowledging during interviews that their understanding and retention of the legal principles was at best marginal, the jury gave a different response on the written questionnaire. They unanimously agreed that they derived an understanding of the purposes of the antitrust laws. Of greater interest is their response to the question, "Did the instructions explain the terms so that you understand how they related to the facts?" Three answered positively to the entire list while the remaining three were positive to all terms except the essential facility doctrine.

b. Student Jury Experiment

A "jury" of six second-semester first-year law students was impaneled to hear the instructions. A law student coached to simulate Judge Krupansky's monotone style read the instructions to the jury. Immediately after completion, the jury was asked to write what they perceived to be correct instructions on monopolization, relevant product and geographic markets, essential facility, proximate cause, and natural monopoly. They were also asked to explain the legal significance of the Miller Incident.

As a group, the student jury flunked, collectively answering the questions 46 percent correctly. They received the highest grades on proximate cause, as might be expected from law students who had recently covered it in Torts. They also received good scores for explaining natural monopoly and relevant geographic market. All jurors drew a blank on the essential facility doctrine; one answered, "I haven't the foggiest," while another commented, "I did hear it mentioned but it slipped by." The answers to the question on the Miller Incident were almost as bad, with only one correct answer.

When asked to explain their inability to retain and comprehend the instructions, the student jury complained of lengthy sentences, repetition, phrasing in the alternative, and boredom from over two hours of listening. One juror summarized the frustration of the group:

> The technical definitions were given in long, almost incomprehensible sentences. The constant rephrasing of definitions was confusing. Also, many of the words used in the definitions were technical.... It became a monotonous mumble-jumble.

c. Jury II

Jury I unanimously approved the suggestion that instructions be given at the beginning, middle, and end of the trial. The theme of this recommendation became reality in Trial II when Judge Krupansky gave oral preliminary instructions and provided the jury with one copy of final instructions for reference during deliberation. (The inability of the parties to resolve differences deterred the use of preliminary instructions in Trial I.)

The preliminary instructions, which summarized the issues, defined terms, and described statutes and alleged violations, got mixed reactions from Jury II. Some jurors felt that early instructions made little, if any, impact, while others said they were helpful. One juror remembered them for the terminology. However, remarks on the effectiveness of final oral instructions raise doubts over the contribution of the preliminary instructions to comprehension.

Reactions to the oral final instructions ranged from "they were difficult to follow" to the thoughts of one juror as she listened: "Oh my God, are we supposed to remember this?" Perhaps because they did get a written copy, the jurors were generally noncommittal on the value of oral instructions.

In general, the "book" (the jury's name for the instructions) inspired confidence. The book was thought to be "helpful," "valuable," and available as a source for definition of rules.

Reliance on the instructions differed among jurors. To a majority, a strong and irrevocable negative impression of the city's case had been formed before deliberation. The jury's rejection of the testimony of the city's two main witnesses, W.H. and Dr. W., their open disgust with what was perceived as repetitious testimony, and the perception that Muny mismanagement was conceded and proven by the city's own witnesses support this conclusion. According to the foreman: "Once the city rested its case, in my mind, because I didn't see anything against antitrust...they could have stopped the trial because they didn't have to go any further." Later he said: "That's what I said when the city rested its case at that point. I'm looking at Lansdale [CEI lead counsel] and I said, 'You bring up any witnesses, I'm going to kill you' [laughing]."

Another juror revealed that since the city had failed to prove its case, the instructions were unnecessary. "That's the way I felt. I think that some of the others felt that way also. I guess that's a formality you have to go through."

Two jurors made constant use of the book during deliberation. Their reliance gravitated toward three areas: "preponderance of the evidence and credibility of witnesses," the "purpose of the Sherman Act," and a description of the corporate organization of CEI and Muny. According to one juror, "when I read preponderance...that's what did it for me. That was the key thing." She continued:

> [T]here's got to be more to it than this, because why else would the city...bring a lawsuit of this size against CEI? You feel like they forgot something, like I said before, they forgot a witness or something, because something is missing. They didn't prove it...we're not to find out what they forgot and what they didn't come up with, we are here to give a verdict with the preponderance of the evidence. If you use that, and that is what the judge told us to use, then we can't find them guilty.

Preponderance of the evidence was given a broad definition, subsuming the credibility of witnesses (the city's witnesses were "goofballs") and the perceived quality of the city lawyers ("not only were the witnesses bad, but their lawyers were bad"). Her gravitation to the section on Sherman Act objectives is consistent with this juror's commitment to a premium on aggressive competition, as expressed throughout interviews. Her interest in the description in the instructions on Muny's corporate status as part of the municipal structure and that it is managed by publicly elected and appointed officials suggests rationalization of a pretrial ideological inclination:

QUESTION: What significance does that have to you?
ANSWER: Well, the fact that they were elected and appointed public officials. I don't really necessarily like the idea of politics [in business].

d. Readability Measurement

Even assuming access and total commitment to utilization of instructions by the jury, the comprehensibility issue remains. The problem is that jurors may not understand what they read. One way of obtaining further insights on this issue is to employ readability tests to determine whether a juror, having read the instructions, could have understood their meaning.

A readability formula is a predictive device designed to furnish an estimation of "the probable success a reader will have in reading and understanding a piece of writing."[146] Dr. E.M. Nicholson, director of the Learning Center at Cleveland State University, conducted readability studies of the instructions and interrogatories used in Trials I and II.

Dr. Nicholson applied the Dale-Chall Formula, considered "consistently more accurate than others."[147] Dale-Chall essentially relies on two counts: average sentence length and the relative number of words not found in the Dale list of three thousand common words.[148] In addition, Dr. Nicholson evaluated the lexical and syntactic complexity of style to determine "comprehension level, concentration, and tracking skills required, and interest background level."[149] The results are measured in terms of readability according to grade levels. The average person reads at the eighth to tenth grade levels.[150]

(i) Instructions: Trial I

Sentence length ranged from 72 to 127 words. While twentieth century American prose averages around 21 words per sentence, the instructions averaged 102.

The study distinguished and measured readability of general vocabulary words and special words (the latter are the nomenclature of a particular discipline, such as antitrust). The former read at eleventh to fourteenth grade levels, the latter would require a twentieth grade education. "The interrelations of syntax and semantics are involved and complicated thereby seriously affecting the level of comprehension for the reader or listener."[151]

The study also measured language-thought sentence structure. The placement of words such as verbs, adjectives, and subjects determines whether a reader can *track* or understand the meaning of the sentence. The longer a sentence, the greater the likelihood that word placement will inhibit tracking by leading to inaccuracies in word recognition, reduced understanding, and loss of reading speed. The study notes that complex language-thought structure "leads to other functional performance losses, *i.e.*, memory (short and long term), retention, attention span, loss of interest and reduced skills of conceptualization."[152] The study rated the instructions' complexity of language-thought sentence structure at the 16.8 grade level.

(ii) Special Interrogatories: Trial I

Ranging from twenty-six words to sixty-six words per sentence, the average sentence contained forty-six words. The language-thought sentence structure came close to the sixteenth grade level. General vocabulary word difficulty rated between the eleventh and thirteenth grade levels but ranked at the twentieth grade level for special words.

Instructions 63

Dr. Nicholson summarized:

> Based on the findings from a thorough analysis of the document provided in the court case of the City of Cleveland versus the Cleveland Electric Illuminating Company, it is reasonable to conclude that the level of difficulty would require jurors with a *minimum* of a high school education plus three years of college. Special instructions beyond those provided in the JURY INSTRUCTIONS would be necessary if the jurors are expected to respond to the specific vocabulary in an intelligent manner. The present definitions are unclear to the "average" juror. In addition, the complexity of the sentence-language-thought structure prohibits and/or diminishes the receiver's ability to follow (track) in order to understand. It should be noted that the average sentence length for twentieth century American prose is approximately twenty (20) to twenty-two (22) words.[153]

(iii) Evaluation of Trial II Instructions and Special Interrogatories

Dr. Nicholson applied the same tests but used a broader sample.[154] In addition to evaluating twenty randomly selected passages, she analyzed ninety-eight selected passages from the final instructions. She also evaluated the material to determine the concentration and tracking skills needed for comprehending the terms.

Sentence length was significantly below Trial I instructions; sentences ranged from 25 to 85 words, and the average length was 52.3 words. It is thus interesting to note that the complexity of language-thought for the Trial II instructions increased one grade level to 17.9. The difficulty of general vocabulary remained essentially the same at the fourteenth grade level, while special words "rated at a level commensurate with no less than one year of formal education in law school and/or legal language type of instructional programs in a post-secondary program."[155] Memory load and retention was scored at the same twentieth grade level.

Dr. Nicholson noted the negative effect of passages used to amplify or clarify and introduced by "stated differently" or "to further explain." This confuses the reader "since new and/or additional legal terms are introduced and what might have been understood, now become more confusing."[156]

Dr. Nicholson concluded that a master's degree grade level or beyond was necessary to conceptualize the instructions. She noted that readability is subverted by the burden of recalling and remembering arcane legal definitions for subsequent application:

> This is an unreasonable expectation for any individual who has not been exposed...in his or her past educational experience to those terms which are peculiar only to that of the legal profession. In addition, the complexity of the sentence-language-thought structure strictly prohibits and/or diminishes the receiver's ability to follow from the beginning of a sentence

through to the end of the sentence in order to adequately comprehend for judgmental purposes.[157]

e. Psycholinguistic Study

As interest in comprehensibility of instructions grows, new measuring techniques are utilized. One of the more promising techniques is psycholinguistics, which is designed to measure comprehension and to identify linguistic factors that cause comprehension difficulties. The "first empirical, objective linguistic study"[158] of instruction comprehensibility, conducted by the Charrows, relied on the paraphrase task technique. Subjects listened to tape recordings of California standard civil jury instructions and then paraphrased their understanding of the material. According to the Charrows, "the validity of the paraphrase task as a measure of comprehensibility rests on the premise that a subject will not be able to paraphrase accurately material that he or she has not understood."[159]

A psycholinguistic evaluation of the *Cleve. v. CEI* instructions was modeled on the Charrow technique. The instructions were divided into eight sections: preponderance of evidence, elements of monopolization, monopoly power, willful acquisition or maintenance of monopoly power, duty to serve and essential facility doctrine, proximate cause, natural monopoly, and damages. Twelve second-year law students read a brief description of the case and then participated in a paraphrasing task. The "jurors" were divided into two juries; Jury I was allowed to hear a tape of the instructions two times while Jury II read the instructions once before paraphrasing.

Each of the eight subjects was broken down into grading units. Each unit consisted of a descriptive phrase or clause. Answers were graded "correct," "correct by inference," or "wrong." The overall average score of correct answers for all elements of the eight sections was 47.7 percent for Jury I and 42.3 percent for Jury II. The average scores for each section were as follows:

	Jury I (%)	Jury II (%)
Proximate cause	63.9	55.6
Monopolization (elements)	60.0	46.7
Preponderance of evidence	55.6	39.5
Monopolization (willful acquisition)	54.4	50.0
Natural monopoly	39.4	34.8
Damages	39.2	40.0
Monopoly power	38.2	37.3
Duty to serve (bottleneck monopoly)	31.2	34.4

Selecting the threshold score of sufficient comprehensibility necessarily relies on an arbitrary judgment. The analysis is evaluative and descriptive and does not provide definitive evidence of comprehension. "The ability of a juror to comprehend a given set of instructions depends on factors in addition to the linguistic construction and vocabulary of the instructions. The context provided by the trial itself may influence the comprehensibility of the charge."[160] Nevertheless, even by generous standards, it is evident that there are serious comprehension problems in the *Cleve. v. CEI* instructions. At the least, the results confirm Dr. Nicholson's conclusion that it requires someone with a postgraduate education to conceptualize the instructions.

Notes

1. 15 USC §§ 1, 2 (1976). The complaint named four defendants in addition to CEI: Duquesne Light Company, Ohio Edison Company, Pennsylvania Power Company, and the Toledo Edison Company. Civil Action 75560, United States District Court for the Northern District of Ohio, July 1, 1975.
2. *Plaintiff City of Cleveland Trial Brief* 5 n.1, July 11, 1980. "Under the agreement, the city received $1.5 million, technical assistance for Muny Light and help in finding expert witnesses for the case against CEI." Cleveland Press, October 9, 1981.
3. Cleveland Plain Dealer, Oct. 10, 1981, p. 22-A.
4. Cleveland Press, Oct. 10, 1981, p. A-17.
5. Much of the historical information is derived from: *Plaintiff City of Cleveland Trial Brief*, July 11, 1980; *Principal Trial Memorandum of Defendant The Cleveland Electric Illuminating Company*, September 20, 1980; Plaintiff's Exhibit 3106 (history of Muny-CEI relationship by Elmer Lindseth, CEI president 1945-60); E. Kenealy, The Cleveland Municipal Light Plant (1935). *See generally*, Kellman, Marino, *City of Cleveland v. CEI: A Case Study In Attempts to Monopolize By Regulated Utilities*, 30 Cleve. St. L. Rev. 5 (1981).
6. The rapid growth was undoubtedly due to Muny's low rate of three cents per kilowatt-hour which had been instituted by Mayor Tom Johnson, Cleveland's populist mayor, who used the low rate to gain support for a campaign to force independent street car firms to charge a three-cent fare. Plaintiff's Exhibit 3106 at I-7.

    By ordinance, city council imposed a three-cent rate on CEI. After hearings and appeals before the Public Utilities Commission, CEI accepted a compromise ordinance which imposed a five-cent rate. R. Hellman, Government Competition in the Electric Utility Industry 303 (1972).
7. In 1945, E.J. Kenealy, Muny engineer and advocate of municipal power, was quoted as noting that "the Municipal Plant was an active competitor of CEI during its early history, but for over 20 years its value in this respect has been one of a threat of competition rather than active competition." Plaintiff's Exhibit 3106 at II-5.
8. *See generally*, Harrison, *Yardstick Competition: A Prematurely Discarded Form of Regulatory Relief*, 53 Tul. L. Rev. 465 (1979).

9. Plaintiff's Exhibit 3106 at III.
10. "When operating interconnected, loss of generating capacity on one system is shared instantaneously by both systems through flow of energy over the interconnecting tie-line that joins the two systems." Plaintiff's Exhibit 3106 at V-1.
11. Second Amended Complaint filed by City of Cleveland, June 9, 1980, at 4.
12. Plaintiff's Trial Brief at 34.
13. According to the city's scenario, rate equalization would terminate Muny's primary competitive advantage in rates "and the stage would have been set for the later acquisition of Muny Light by CEI, consistent with the conclusions reached in the comprehensive CEI study of successful acquisition of municipal systems by privately-owned companies." Plaintiff's Trial Brief at 30.

"It was this attitude that permeated MELP's administration for the next 40 or more years, namely, that synchronous interconnection with CEI would somehow result in loss of independence for MELP and result in MELP's becoming a distribution utility rather than a completely integrated one." Plaintiff's Exhibit 3106 at V-3. Moreover, a city council special committee "prophesized that if MELP bought power from CEI, MELP would not modernize its own equipment and ultimately would provide only a distribution function and then be sold to CEI for its residual value." Id. at V-18. See Plaintiff's Trial Brief at 32.
14. Plaintiff's Trial Brief at 32. The city also charged that in 1972, CEI adopted the policy of providing load transfers only in power outages and refused to provide power to enable Muny to perform essential maintenance and repairs. Id. at 33.
15. Stokes was originally in favor of selling the plant (R. Hellman, *supra* note 6 at 307) but hired Mr. Warren Hinchee as commissioner of Muny Light to improve the system. "Hinchee, an electrical engineer, accountant and adamant proponent of public power, took on CEI and spearheaded City attempts to get a permanent electrical hookup with CEI and to get the company to relay cheap out-of-state power to Muny Light." Cleveland Plain Dealer, October 9, 1981.
16. Federal Power Commission, Opinion No. 644-13, May 9, 1977.
17. Plaintiff's Trial Brief at 34. The permanent interconnection became operational in May, 1975. The regulatory hearing led to the antitrust litigation.

> Lawyers for the city, in preparing for hearings before the AEC, now known as the Nuclear Regulatory Commission, obtained numerous internal CEI documents and questioned CEI officials under oath.
> Based on what they had learned, the lawyers recommended to the city that an antitrust suit be filed in an effort to collect damages.

Cleveland Plain Dealer, Oct. 9, 1981.
18. "The bitter struggle between the city and the Cleveland Electric Illuminating Co., shrouded in a seven-year-old cloud of litigation and political debate, pits

the advocates of two antagonistic principles: private enterprise and public ownership." Cleveland Plain Dealer, Jan. 29, 1978, p. 1.
19. Ohio Const. Art. XVIII, § 4.
20. Ohio Rev. Code § 5709.08 (property tax); § 5727.05 (excise and franchise tax).
21. Ohio Rev. Code § 4905.02. See generally, Vanbel, *Municipal Home Rule in Ohio*, 3 Ohio N.U.L. Rev. 1375, pt. V (1976).
22. Ohio Const. Art. XVIII, § 4.
23. See Kellman and Marino, *supra* note 5.
24. City of Cleveland v. CEI, Presiding Examiner's Initial Decision in Consolidated Proceedings, Docket E-7631, E-7633, July 12, 1972, p. 1.
25. "Every person who shall monopolize, or attempt to monopolize, or combine or conspire with any other person or persons, to monopolize any part of the trade, or commerce among the several states [violates § 2]." 15 U.S.C. § 2 (1976).
26. 15 U.S.C. § 15 (1976) provides that "[a]ny person who shall be injured in his business or property by reason of anything forbidden in the antitrust laws may sue...and shall recover threefold the damages by him sustained, and the cost of the suit, including a reasonable attorney's fee."
27. Plaintiff's Trial Brief at 42. See Austin, *City of Cleveland v. Cleveland Electric Illuminating Company: Monopolization, Regulation and Natural Monopoly*, 13 U. Toledo L. Rev. 611 (1982).
28. U.S. v. E.I. duPont de Nemours Co., 351 U.S. 377, 391 (1956). Plaintiff's Trial Brief at 57.
29. Since 1967 CEI has been a member of the Central Area Power Coordination Group (CAPCO), a cooperative group of investor-owned utilities. Other members of this power pool are Pennsylvania Power Company, Duquesne Light Company, Ohio Edison, and Toledo Edison.

 The city argued that CEI's market power was embellished by qualitative factors such as CAPCO membership, control of an extensive transmission network, and other barriers to entry that gave CEI the requisite market power to control prices and exclude competition. Plaintiff's Trial Brief at 60-1.
30. Jury instructions, Record at 19196. Jury I chose the city of Cleveland, plus a contiguous area. CEI controlled over 80 percent of retail sales in this market. Jury II settled on the thirty square miles of direct competition where CEI had less than 60 percent of sales.
31. Plaintiff's Trial Brief at 65.
32. Plaintiff's Trial Brief at 67.
33. See U.S. v. Griffith, 334 U.S. 100 (1948). In a supplemental trial brief the city described the legal effects of the Muny Displacement Program:

Whether such acts in and of themselves would have violated Section 2 is not important. What is important is for the jury to consider these acts in light of the fact that they were committed by a company possessing monopoly power and they were aimed at that company's sole competitor. Thus, contrary to CEI's assertions, both the unfair competitive acts themselves, and the exclusionary intent with which they were undertaken, are relevant to a proper resolution of this case.

City of Cleveland's Supplemental Trial Brief at 15.

34. Stipulation 231-39.

35. The Miller Incident will be discussed in greater detail *infra*.

36. According to a CEI study, price parity with a municipal system usually resulted in acquisition by the investor-owned utility. See note 13, *supra*.

37. Record at 12941.

38. Record at 11269, 11278. In addition, a principal city witness testified that CEI threatened to disconnect the load transfers (which supplied Muny with emergency power) within three days unless the city paid all outstanding CEI bills. Record at 11407.

39. Record at 11389.

40. Record at 11559. The city also perceived anticompetitive intention in: CEI's efforts to eliminate private generation of power by industrial firms such as Union Carbide; CEI's refusal to interconnect with the Painesville, Ohio, municipal utility except on rate equalization terms; the use of dead load transfers which caused interrupted service to Muny's customers.

41. Plaintiff's Trial Brief at 70.

42. CEI Opening Statement, Record at 10281.

43. "Indeed, the evidence will uncontrovertibly show that any alleged actions of defendant in this case were necessarily inconsequential in view of MELP's own pervasive and longstanding mismanagement and neglect...." Principal Trial Memorandum of Defendant at 170.

44. U.S. v. Aluminum Co. of America, 148 F.2d 416, 429-30 (2d Cir. 1945).

45. Posner, *Natural Monopoly and its Regulation*, 21 Stan. L. Rev. 548 (1969). *See* A. Kahn, The Economics of Regulation 119-23 (Vol. II, 1971).

46. Principal Trial Memorandum of Defendant at 108.

47. Principal Trial Memorandum of Defendant at 155.

48. Note, *Selection of Jurors by Voir Dire Examination and Challenge*, 58 Yale L.J. 638, 643 n.26 (1949).

49. Dennis Kucinich used the CEI-city issue to help drive Perk from office, only to have fallout from the struggle contribute to his defeat two years later when George Voinovich ousted him. In March 1976, on the eve of the scheduled start of the trial, the Perk administration announced a tentative settlement

of the suit. Under the proposed agreement, CEI would have purchased Muny for $158.5 million. That proposal, however, was opposed by members of council who wanted the city to acquire CEI and expand Muny into a regional power system. The proposed sale became a major issue in the 1977 mayoral campaign as Kucinich characterized CEI as a ruthless giant trying to eliminate its only competition and vowed that he would not sell Muny. Kucinich's Muny Light stance helped topple Perk, who was eliminated from the race in the primary election. Kucinich then defeated Edward Feighan in the general election. Cleveland Press, Oct. 9, 1981, p. 12.

50. Profiles are taken from *voir dire* questionnaires filled out by prospective jurors. The Jury I questionnaire contained fifty-one questions; Jury II answered seventy-two questions.

51. See *supra* note 49.

52. The jury was advised to consider: the city's intention to extend its electric system; its planning and engineering to implement expansion; reasonable probability of obtaining approval of city council; the cost; the ability of the city to finance the expansion; reasonable probability of city council's appropriating the funds; and the reasonable period of time required for completion. Record at 6578.

53. Cleveland Plain Dealer, Sept. 15, 1980, p. 5-A.

54. The juror was referring to defense counsel's closing argument: "Repeatedly, he referred to his client as 'good ol' CEI'." Cleveland Press, Nov. 4, 1980, p. A-7.

55. Record at 15004. See *also* testimony of Karl H. Rudolph, CEI president, 1967–1975, Nov. 4, 1980.

56. Record at 10244.

57. Record at 10247.

58. Special Verdict Form, Cleve. v. CEI, No. C75-560 (N.D. Ohio, filed July 1, 1975).

59. Cleveland Press, Dec. 7, 1980 (editorial).

60. Cleveland Plain Dealer, Sept. 18, 1980, p. 1.

61. Cleveland Press, Sept. 18, 1980, p. A-18. The legal issue was embellished by out-of-court activity: "Yesterday, The Plain Dealer asked John Lansdale, CEI chief lawyer, why CEI had not openly filed the suit. 'None of your business. We had a First Amendment right to do it any goddamn way we pleased,' Lansdale said. Lansdale said what CEI did was comparable to the news media clandestinely obtaining information and then publishing it under protection of the First Amendment." Cleveland Plain Dealer, Sept. 18, 1980, p. 12-A.

The news media continued coverage of the Miller Incident: "Judge Won't Let City Tell Jury CEI Backed Lawsuit," Cleveland Plain Dealer, Sept. 20, 1980, p. 19-A; "CEI Attorney Denies Client Delayed Tie-In," Cleveland Plain

Dealer, Oct. 1, 1980, p. 14-A; "Krupansky To Rethink Ban On Telling Jury of CEI's Suit Scheme," Cleveland Plain Dealer, Oct. 25, 1980, p. 25-A; "CEI Trial Told of Move To Stymie Tie-In," Cleveland Plain Dealer, Oct. 29, 1980, p. 5-A.

62. Joint Stipulation 227-241.
63. Joint Stipulation 230.
64. Joint Stipulation 232.
65. Joint Stipulation 229.
66. Brief of Plaintiff-Appellant at 32 (United States Court of Appeals for the Sixth Circuit).
67. Eastern Railroad Presidents' Conference v. Noerr Motor Freight, Inc., 365 U.S. 127 (1961).
68. United Mine Workers of America v. Pennington, 381 U.S. 657 (1965).
69. Record at 1262.
70. Record at 1261-2.
71. Record at 1263. (Citing United Mine Workers of America v. Pennington, 281 U.S. 657, 670 n.4 [1965].)
72. Record at 1265.
73. "At the first trial of this cause, the court ultimately acceded to plaintiff's request to introduce the evidence incorporated into Stipulations 226 through 241 only after the defendant had affirmatively elicited from its own witnesses during the presentation of the defendant's case-in-chief evidence which compelled the inference that CEI undertook no conduct to impede, hinder or delay the construction of the 69KV temporary emergency interconnection.

"...That is to say, the Court sanctioned the use of *Noerr-Pennington* evidence only after the defendants themselves had 'opened the door' by introducing evidence designed to create, in the minds of the jury, prejudicial inferences which could only be dispelled by the admission of constitutionally protected activity."
Memorandum and Order, Civil Action C75-560, August 17, 1981, p. 8.

The court refused to allow the city to "trigger the admission of the constitutionally protected activity simply by undertaking a course of examination which is solely designed to create an inference which may be dispelled by disclosure of the protected activity." *Id.* at 9.
74. Oral Order of September 19, 1980, Record at 1243-66. This order was held applicable to Trial II by Order of May 18, 1981, at 10, and invoked in Trial II to exclude the stipulations. Order of August 17, 1981, at 8.
75. According to a press description, defense counsel "brushed off the secret Miller suit by telling jurors it lasted only 11 days and didn't work anyway." Cleveland Press, Nov. 4, 1980, p. A-7.

76. Record at 6566–6570.
77. Cleveland Plain Dealer, Aug. 15, 1981, p. 10-A.
78. Cleveland Plain Dealer, Oct. 3, 1981, p. 24-C.
79. A summary of the special interrogatories:
    1. Relevant geographic market of (*a*) "The approximate 30-square miles within the geographic boundaries of the City of Cleveland wherein the electric systems of CEI and Muny Light both served customers," (*b*) "The geographic boundaries of the entire City of Cleveland," (*c*) "Other."
    2. (*a*) Did CEI monopolize the relevant market? (*b*) Did CEI attempt to monopolize the relevant market?
    3. Did CEI's conduct proximately cause damage to business or property of the city of Cleveland?
    4. (*a*) Is the relevant market a natural monopoly? (*b*) If yes, has CEI "monopolized or attempted to monopolize the relevant market by unfair or predatory means?"
    5. Damages: from CEI's refusal to interconnect; from refusal to wheel PASNY power; from the free wiring program. The jury was given three damage periods: July 1971 through 1980, 1981 through 1988, and 1989 through 2000.
80. Cleveland Plain Dealer, Nov. 20, 1980, p. 1.
81. Cleveland Press, Nov. 20, 1980, p. 1.
82. After reviewing the following account of deliberation, the foreman questioned the use of *authoritarian*. She accepted *structured and organized* as accurate.
83. Strawn, Buchanan, Pryor, Taylor, *Reaching A Verdict, Step by Step*, 60 Judicature 383 (1977).
84. *Id.* at 385.
85. If there can be an irony in a hung jury, it is in the holdout's pretrial antagonism toward CEI. "When I read in the paper that this trial was gonna be, I said immediately, oh yea, CEI is definitely guilty... 'cause they [are] charging me like hell. I wanted to cuss 'em. I have to pay through the nose. So, I know they got to be guilty.... But, when I went in as a juror and listened to the evidence...then I changed my mind. Then I said, well, I have to go by the evidence and not by what I feel about my bills."
86. Cleveland Plain Dealer, Nov. 20, 1980, p. 6-A.
87. Cleveland Plain Dealer, Nov. 25, 1980, p. 1.
88. Cleveland Press, Nov. 25, 1980, p. 1.
89. Eventually, council passed a resolution requesting that the mayor continue the case. Cleveland Plain Dealer, Nov. 25, 1980, p. 13-A.
90. Cleveland Plain Dealer, Nov. 27, 1980, p. 16-A.
91. Cleveland Press, Dec. 4, 1980, p. C-5. Henry Eckhart, former PUCO commissioner and a witness at Trial II, accused CEI of "trying to intimidate jurors, who may think twice before recommending a big judgment that they as CEI customers—may have to pay for." Cleveland Plain Dealer, Dec. 4, 1980, p. 1.

92. Cleveland Plain Dealer, Dec. 23, 1980, p. 14-A. The Cleveland Press responded with an editorial entitled, "Don't Move 2d CEI Trial." Cleveland Press, Dec. 24, 1980, p. B-6.
93. Cleveland Plain Dealer, Jan. 9, 1981, p. 7-A.
94. Cleveland Plain Dealer, May 17, 1981, p. 36-A.
95. Cleveland Plain Dealer, May 17, 1981, p. 36-A.
96. National L.J., Aug. 31, 1981, p. 1.
97. *Interview* with James Murphy, CEI counsel, Sept. 14, 1982, at 26.
98. Broeder, *The Impact of the Lawyers: An Informal Appraisal*, 1 Valparaiso L. Rev. 40, 50–52 (1966); Curtin, *Objections*, 8 Litigation 37 (1982).
99. Murphy *Interview, supra* note 97 at 14.
100. Record at 1028.
101. Record at 11498.
102. "During the morning break in U.S. District Court, John Lansdale, CEI's lead lawyer, shouted at William B. Norris, the city's lead lawyer, 'How can you keep asking these leading questions?'

"Norris approached Lansdale and eventually backed him up against a bench, glaring and yelling back. Norris, towering at least six inches above Lansdale, shouted back, 'These are not intentional (leading questions).' Now inches apart, Lansdale barked out, 'Back off.'

"When Norris continued to argue, Lansdale shoved him sharply in the chest with open hands, knocking Norris back several feet. Norris lost his balance and banged into a table.

"Recovering his balance and composure, Norris said, 'I'm glad I didn't hit you.'

"Outside the courtroom, Lansdale cooled off and went over to Norris' courthouse office. Before he entered the room, he told reporters, 'I suppose I'm in trouble with you guys.' As he walked into the room, he said, 'Brad, I want to apologize.'

"Yesterday's confrontation mirrored the previous day's activities, except that U.S. District Judge Robert B. Krupansky threatened the combatants with possible contempt of court charges.

"In nearly comic understatement, he said, 'The court senses a certain degree of tension since the last recess...I request there be no further verbal or physical confrontations in this courtroom.'

"The shouting and pushing incidents happened when the jury was not present." Cleveland Plain Dealer, July 24, 1981, p. 16-C.
103. Murphy *Interview, supra* note 97 at 17.
104. Cleveland Plain Dealer, Oct. 9, 1981, p. 13-A.
105. Murphy *Interview, supra* note 97 at 19.
106. MS. COLEMAN: I tried to sit by, but I must take exception to the—to Mr. Lansdale's yelling at the witness. It is uncalled for and unnecessary.

THE COURT: I hadn't noticed it. You know, you have a very difficult witness, and it is obvious that he is being evasive.

MS. COLEMAN: I take exception to that.

THE COURT: You are perfectly free to take exception to my remarks. I am just telling you my impression.

My impression is that I can comment in my charge if I am desirous of doing it, and I am telling you my impressions of this witness's testimony.

Now, you are perfectly free to take exception, but you know, I might say this, Mr. Lansdale: Your questions leave something to be desired. They are so involved that it is difficult to follow, number one, and number two, if the witness would listen to the questions and answer the questions, I think that the entire proceeding would move along.

And if you have any objections to questions, you are free to make them, but if you don't make objections, then your associates shouldn't complain.

Record at 3984-5.

107. Cleveland Plain Dealer, Aug. 26, 1981, p. 6-A.
108. Record at 14948.
109. Murphy *Interview, supra* note 97 at 28.
110. Early testimony on mismanagement surprised defense counsel who viewed it as a fundamental mistake on the plaintiff's part. Murphy *Interview, supra* note 97 at 15, 28.
111. Record at 10433.
112. Record at 10626.
113. Record at 10763.
114. Record at 10757.
115. Record at 10793.
116. Record at 10793.
117. Record at 10863.
118. Record at 11047.
119. Record at 11047.
120. Record at 15918.
121. *See* Austin, *City of Cleveland v. Cleveland Electric Illuminating Co.: Monopolization, Regulation and Natural Monopoly,* 13 U. Toledo L. Rev. 609, 644–49 (1982).
122. Several jurors did, however, remember the style and demeanor of Professor O'Donnell, CEI's chief economic expert on natural monopoly.
123. Rule 51, Fed. Rules of Civil Procedure.
124. W. Mathes, E. Devitt, Federal Jury Practice and Instructions § 5.05 (1965).
125. Instructions, Record at 19166. "A question of fact usually calls for proof. A question of law usually calls for argument." Morris, *Law and Fact,* 55 Harv. L. Rev. 1303, 1304 (1942).
126. Schwarzer, *Communicating With Juries: Problems and Remedies,* 69 Calif. L. Rev. 731, 734 (1981).
127. Spark v. U.S., 156 U.S. 51, 80-2 (1895).

128. Schwarzer, *supra* note 126 at 736. The author adds: "The process of trying cases thus became more burdensome for courts, counsel, and the parties. Reform was badly needed and came through the development of pattern instruction." *Id.*
129. Preliminary Instruction, Record at 10153.
130. There are stylistic and substantive differences between the instructions. The syntax and structure of Instructions II were tighter and long paragraphs were broken down into shorter paragraphs. Substantive changes included: no reference to CAPCO; exclusion of the Miller Incident; jury advised not to consider in determining relevant market possible influence of CEI prices; PUCO's authority was "properly and effectively exercised"; jury advised to consider effect of PUCO's authority on CEI's market power; FPC criteria for requiring interconnection different from those adopted here; no damages allowable from failure of eighty-five megawatt operator; jury to consider possible future losses and same use formula to account for inflation and discount of present value.
131. Record at 19201.
132. Record at 19197. In determining the relevant geographic market, the jury was given these factors to consider:
   1. The city's intention to expand beyond the existing area of competitive overlap.
   2. Existence of planning and engineering to expand beyond existing facilities.
   3. Probability of obtaining council approval.
   4. Cost of expansion.
   5. Ability of city to finance expansion.
   6. Probability of council appropriating funds.
   7. Reasonable period of time for expansion.
133. Record at 19205.
134. Record at 19207.
135. Record at 19213.
136. Record at 19218.
137. Record at 19218.
138. Record at 19219.
139. Record at 19200.
140. Record at 19200.
141. Record at 19221.
142. Record at 19240.
143. Record at 19241.
144. Record at 19242-3.
145. Record at 19244.
146. G. Klare, Measurement of Readability 34 (1963).
147. G. Klare, *supra* note 146 at 22.

148. Dale & Chall, *A Formula for Predicting Readability*, Bureau of Educational Research, Ohio State Univ., reprinted from 27 Ed. Research Bull. 1127 (1948). The Flesch formula, developed contemporaneously with that of Dale and Chall, is based on average sentence length and average word length by number of syllables. R. Flesch, How to Test Readability (1951). *See also* Foulger, *A Simplified Flesch Formula*, 55 Journalism Quarterly 167 (1978).
149. *The City of Cleveland Versus The Cleveland Electric Illuminating Company: A Quantitative Estimate of the Readability Level of the Written Material Provided the Jurors By Judge Krupansky*, March 18, 1981, p. 2.
150. *Id.* at 3.
151. *Id.* at 3.
152. *Id.* at 2.
153. *Id.* at 4.
154. *Id.* at 4.
155. *Id.* at 3.
156. *Id.* at 3.
157. *Id.* at 4–5.
158. Charrow and Charrow, *Making Legal Language Understandable: A Psycholinguistic Study of Jury Instructions*, 79 Colum. L. Rev. 1306, 1307 (1979). *See also* A. Elwork, B. Sales, J. Alfini, Making Jury Instructions Understandable (1982).
159. Charrow and Charrow, *supra* note 158 at 1310.
160. Charrow and Charrow, *supra* note 158 at 1317.

Part III
Introduction: Defining and Predicting Complexity

> Except in an experimental setting, the accuracy of predictions of case complexity too great for jury comprehension can never be verified.
> —*Protracted Civil Trials:*
> *Views From the Bench and Bar* 9 (1981)

Dissenting in *In re Japanese Elect. Prod. Antitrust Lit.*, Judge Gibbons declared that while there may be a case too complex for a jury to comprehend, "it is inconceivable to me that it could be recognized as such in the absence of a trial record."[1] He rejected the majority's criteria (or any criteria) as being inadequate for making *a priori* judgments on complexity. Nonetheless, he assumed that a trial record could be dispositive of the complexity issue.

Whether the existence of a trial record provides a credible means of determining complexity has three ramifications. First, in second trials, either from hung juries or other reasons, the court would enjoy the obvious advantage of having a transcript to evaluate, the chance to talk to counsel, and perhaps the results of a jury poll.[2] Secondly, as trial records are evaluated and characterized as complex or not, a body of precedent would be compiled and other courts confronted with second trial motions to strike could make more reliable judgments. Finally, *posterior* analysis of trial records may supply benchmarks and insights to justify—or negate—the credibility of *a priori* decisions on complexity.

The jury survey, derived from the two trial experiences of *Cleve. v. CEI*, constitutes a resource for exploring these ramifications and for reaching conclusions on defining and predicting complexity.

1. A Priori Characterization

Cleve. v. CEI is a borderline case for *a priori* classification as being too complex for jury comprehension. Neither the city or CEI counsel perceived usual problems that would require extraordinary treatment under the Manual for Complex Litigation.[3] The indicia of complexity available for projection did not measure up to that existing in *In re Japanese Elect. Prod. Antitrust Lit.* Except for the engineering intricacies of synchronous interconnection, technology did not appear as burdensome or difficult as that of manufacturing television components. By the time the case went to trial, multiple parties were not involved, nor was the existence of an international conspiracy at issue.

On the other hand, substantively difficult legal issues could be anticipated. In addition to the complexities and "thorny law"[4] of monopolization, relevant market, and so forth, the case involved the extremely difficult legal-economic issue of market power in a regulated industry and the equally complex but also novel defense of natural monopoly. Moreover, the refusal to deal allegations fell within what the Sixth Circuit calls the most "conceptually difficult"[5] activity of a monopolist seeking to vertically integrate.

Despite the novelty of some of the issues, *Cleve.* v. *CEI* is not a likely candidate for an *a priori* projection as too complex for a jury. Courts have yet to grant a motion to strike merely because Sherman section 2 allegations were involved.

2. Posterior Complexity

In researching jury comprehension, the Federal Judicial Center recognized four possible problem areas: protraction (trial length); and three forms of complexity: managerial, factual, and legal.[6] To determine *posterior* complexity, *Cleve.* v. *CEI* will be evaluated under each category.

a. Protraction

Protraction can be measured by trial days, trial hours per day, and elapsed time from opening statements to deliberation. A judgment as to what constitutes protracted litigation is necessarily arbitrary. Since jurors must be present for a full day's work regardless of actual trial time, number of trial days is arguably the most revealing indicator of the possible effects on jurors.[7]

The Administrative Office of the United States Courts uses nineteen trial days as the threshold for protracted litigation. Both trials exceeded this threshold; Trial I lasted twenty-nine trial days over two months' elapsed time and Trial II consumed fifty-nine trial days over a four-month period.[8]

Length can adversely affect comprehension in two ways: (1) it can reduce the effectiveness of memory, and (2) it can create personal problems that distract juror commitment. The majority of jurors did not complain of personal hardships in serving or that their employment had been adversely affected. Two alternates, one from each jury, were extremely bitter about the experience. One alternate refused to be interviewed, the other declined to discuss the reasons for her displeasure except to note that "things were never explained." A member of Jury II complained of the cost and time of travel and seriously considered asking to be excused. Overall, however,

Introduction 79

all jurors and alternates evidenced a sense of camaraderie and many jurors continued to communicate long after the trials. (Jury II conducts an annual reunion.)

Jurors did acknowledge that length adversely affected retention of testimony. Early testimony and identity of witnesses were forgotten. There were "too many witnesses" and "no way" could the "average" juror retain the testimony. Generally, Jury II was more confident of memory with several members using selective memory on "important" witnesses. The common refrain of Jury II was that the trial was "tedious" and "boring." Noting that a photographic memory was necessary, an alternate complained that "it's an exercise in self-discipline to just sit there day after day, hour after hour, and to be plunged into a world that's totally foreign."

b. Managerial Complexity

The Federal Judicial Center states that "managerial complexity grows with the number of parties and the geographical distances between their home bases."[9] *Cleve. v. CEI* was a local trial involving only two parties, both competing in the same geographical market, and both with home offices in Cleveland. The proximity of law firms and litigants to the court resulted in efficient document storage and retrieval. As a result, managerial complexity was not a problem.

The major problem areas in *Cleve. v. CEI* involved fact and conceptual (substantive) difficulty.

Fact-finding by the Jury in Antitrust Litigation

1. Fact-finding Process and Types of Facts

Under prevailing convention, the court supplies the rules of law in the instructions while the jury determines the facts and renders a verdict consistent with the law.[10] Typically, facts produce effects to which the instructions assign legal significance.[11] A runs a red light at an excessive rate of speed, strikes B, and breaks B's legs. The event has produced facts which the jury can quantify into effects and then determine the rights and duties of the parties in accordance with the rules of applicable tort law.

In antitrust, the jury is confronted with a much more complicated task. They must first ascertain the primary facts, the "raw elements of the case."[12] An example of a primary fact is the allegation that CEI instituted a customer conversion strategy with the objective of using sales ploys such as free wiring to attract customers away from Muny. Likewise, the negotiations surrounding interconnection are primary facts. Primary facts also included the technology of interconnection and the history of the industry. Most litigation, such as tort and contract, is dominated by primary facts. In antitrust litigation, the jury must also assimilate economic facts. Economic facts are judgments or interpretations as to the economic effect or significance of primary facts. In antitrust litigation, economic facts will generally concern some facet of market structure and performance.[13] An example of an economic fact is the natural monopoly defense raised by CEI. Relying on primary facts describing the characteristics of the structure of the Cleveland market, CEI's expert economist concluded that a natural monopoly existed, and thus, as a matter of economics, only one firm could efficiently serve the public. Another example is Dr. W.'s interpretation of CEI's customer conversion strategy as a type of destructive competition inimical to the best interests of the marketplace and harmful to Muny.

The final step is to relate the primary and economic facts to legal rules. The Sherman Act defines the prohibited effects (to monopolize) and the instructions identify the elements of the violation. In resolving *Cleve.* v.

CEI, the jury had to process primary facts, economic facts, and then determine whether the proscribed liability effects were produced.[14] In the process, they had to determine two important law or procedural facts: preponderance of the evidence and proximate cause. This is not an easy task.

> Antitrust law and economics are both concerned with business facts—with individual company activities and relations among companies and their effect upon the market freedom of others and the consuming public. Although these facts are the same whether viewed from a legal or an economic standpoint, unfortunately their effects often are not susceptible of direct proof and hence conclusions as to these effects often must depend upon inferences or conclusions drawn from these facts which are susceptible of direct proof. Thus, it is often impossible to show the precise effect which a given course of conduct may have upon competition.[15]

2. Comprehension: Jury I
a. Primary Facts

The primary facts of *Cleve. v. CEI* fall into three broad categories: historical, technological, and behavioral. The evolution of the two utility systems, the ebbs and tides of the rivalry, a profile of management attitudes, and politics comprised history. Technological facts included the electronics of interconnection, electricity generation and transmission, plus other engineering concepts. Most primary facts described behavior, such as negotiations surrounding the interconnection and the refusal to wheel power, the customer conversion strategy, and the cluster of dirty tricks allegedly performed by CEI.

Jury I complained that comprehension was impeded by lack of memory; it was a long trial in which the testimony became a blur. Nevertheless, Jury I appeared to have remembered and understood a wide range of primary facts. They were familiar with the history of the rivalry and remembered the testimony of city witnesses describing Muny's struggle to compete with CEI. Plaintiff's Exhibit 3106, a historical overview of the Muny–CEI conflict, was read in part or totally by the jurors and the "correct" interpretation was a source of dispute with the dissenter during deliberation.

The jurors had a general understanding of the technology. They understood much of the terminology, such as wheeling and synchronous interconnection. They were likely aided by the experience of one juror, a retired welder who acted as the "expert." The foreman's description of an exchange between the expert juror and the dissenter over dead load interconnection suggests that the latter had difficulty with technology:

> [She] had H. so confused one time about power that was bought. She said that if power went out in those lines running in front of your house and lines running across the street that all you had to do was just more or less go over there and get some power from that line across the street.

QUESTION: How?
ANSWER: That's what H. ...we never did get [that] out of her and H. said, "Well, is it like you just take a bucket?" [Laughing] And I remember that to the day, H. was so frustrated, well, you just can't take a bucket over there and fill it up. He said, "If it is water or something like that you could go get some, but you can't put electricity in a bucket," and she said, "Well, not exactly a bucket," but she says, "You can just go over there and hook into the line and just bring it over to your house." She said, "You know, you could go over there with a pair of pliers and just attach something onto that line and it will come into your house."

Jury I was knowledgeable about the facts of behavior. Retention of testimony relating to this fact category was good and they understood the conduct allegations and counterallegations exchanged by the witnesses. As expected, in interviews they emphasized testimony about conduct perceived as favorable to the city's case. W.H., the city's principal witness on CEI's behavior on interconnection, made a strong impression. Moreover, the jury felt confident about their knowledge of conduct facts which fit into their perception of what the case was all about: who did what to whom.

b. Economic Facts

Jury I's memory was locked into conduct facts. When the questioning shifted to economic facts, the responses became noncommittal, evasive, or, at times, acknowledgement of noncomprehension. There is absolutely no indication that the jurors understood economic facts such as market power. The most dramatic evidence of noncomprehension was the purchase of a dictionary during deliberation to look up *relevant* (market) and *monopoly*. (One juror could not pronounce *relevant*.) At one point during deliberation, several jurors assumed that to have a monopoly a firm must control 100 percent of the market. There was no comprehension of the economic facts of the essential facility doctrine. They had very little understanding of the role of regulation as demonstrated by the remark that CEI could never go out of business since "they can always go to [PUCO] and get more money."

Natural monopoly was beyond the jury's comprehension. Not only did the jurors not understand the concept, but they seemed to resent CEI for advancing the principle that in some markets only one firm can survive and efficiently serve the market. They considered this assertion as another manifestation of CEI's bad attitude. It is interesting that CEI's expert witness on natural monopoly generated the strongest negative feelings of any witness.

Fact-finding by the Jury 83

3. *Comprehension: Jury II*
a. *Primary Facts*
Historical facts dominated the jurors' memories of the testimony. Conversation invariably turned to examples of Muny mismanagement, and to testimony describing power outages, reliability problems, poor maintenance, politics, and fiscal problems. The city's witness on history, Elmer Lindseth, CEI's president from 1945 to 1960, made a strong and positive impression on the jury. He was seen as the ideal executive: firm, confident, and knowledgeable—a father-figure. Hence, Jury II possessed a thorough knowledge of history, albeit with their own interpretation.

The jurors were generally knowledgeable of and conversant with electrical utility technology. They knew the technology of interconnection and understood concepts such as dead load transfers and synchronous power exchange. They described various events in the vocabulary of the industry.

The members of Jury II knew the details of the conduct allegations and enjoyed discussing—and rejecting—the city's version of what occurred. In particular, they were knowledgeable about the testimony of W.H., a key plaintiff witness.

b. *Economic Facts*
Jury II's fixation on Muny mismanagement makes it difficult to get an accurate appraisal on their comprehension of economic facts. Since Muny's problems were assumed to be self-inflicted, the jury either ignored or never reached some of the economic issues. Questions on monopolization or bottleneck monopoly were deflected by references to mismanagement, political interference, or other perceived wrongs attributed to Muny. Dr. W., who explained the economic terms and the economic effects of CEI's behavior, was held in such disdain that the jurors virtually ignored his testimony.

Perhaps because it was a CEI defense, the jury recollected the natural monopoly argument. (The defense's economic expert made a favorable impression.) It was quite clear, however, that they did not comprehend the economics of natural monopoly.

Although they evidenced very modest, if any, familiarity with economic facts, Jury II imposed its own preconceived version of competition on history and conduct. It was classic laissez faire in which the "invisible hand" had plenty of freedom to function. Competition assumes aggressive sales tactics like CEI's customer conversion strategy and disdains any obligation by one firm to aid a less efficient rival.

4. Instructions

The instructions describe the legal rules applicable to primary and economic facts. The responsibility of the jury is to identify and evaluate those facts that are germane to a rule or an element of a rule. The successful achievement of this task assumes comprehension of both facts and rules of law.

The longstanding and often intuitive assumption that communication static between judge and jury inhibits or precludes comprehension of instructions is being confirmed by research. According to a federally funded study, "the average juror may understand only about 50 percent of the instructions...[and] there is a high probability that many verdicts reflect misunderstanding of the jurors' role, their individual beliefs about the facts of the case, and, in many instances, about what the law requires."[16]

a. Jury I

My interpretation and analysis of interviews with the jurors of Jury I (including alternates) is that their comprehension level of the instructions was very low, if not nonexistent. The foreman summarized for her colleagues by acknowledging that she did not remember the oral instructions as she entered deliberation. Having experienced with Jury I the court's oral presentation of the rules, I can empathize and confirm the memory and comprehension problems. Reporters in attendance took copious notes, only to discover they were incomprehensible.

Several events dramatize the serious ramifications of noncomprehension. Even after a recharge by the court on proximate cause, the jury failed to understand the law, instead adopting a broad and incorrect rule: "Did CEI hurt Muny?" In addition, there was the Miller Incident, concerning CEI's covert use of a third party to file a lawsuit against Muny. It was admitted in evidence by Judge Krupansky for purposes of possible impeachment of CEI witnesses. Either failing to remember the instructions or not understanding the technical restrictions attached to the consideration of this evidence, several jurors viewed it as either an antitrust violation or as more of CEI's bad conduct.

Isolated from rules of law, the jurors sought to render a decision consistent with intuition and personal interpretation of testimony:

> QUESTION: How can you resolve a case if you don't know what the law is...?
> ANSWER: Well...the only answer I would give you to that would be...weighing the evidence and determining which side you thought was right.

b. Jury II

Preliminary instructions furnish jurors with a preface to the case, enabling them more effectively to comprehend and evaluate evidence. The assumption is that "[w]hen given instructions as to what materials they are expected to learn, people will learn it more effectively by concentrating on the relevant material and paying less attention to irrelevant material."[17] Informed of the relevant material at the beginning of the trial, the jurors will presumably give it high priority.

The overall impression from interviews is that preliminary instructions had, at best, modest impact. There is no indication that they helped jurors channel attention to relevant testimony and they clearly did not enhance retention and comprehension of economic facts. Indeed, their content restricted efficiency; the description of issues, terms, and violations was either too abstract or irrelevant for the jury to relate to primary and economic facts. For example, the instructions did not mention mismanagement, a theme that dominated the trial.

Research indicates that access to written instructions during deliberation are preferable to oral instructions; jurors spend more than twice as much time "applying the law" and are "more efficient" and engage in "higher quality deliberations."[18] Jury II's experience does not support this assumption.

By the time the city rested its case, four jurors had decided that the city had no case against CEI and that Muny's demise in the retail electricity market was its own fault. According to the foreman, "once the city rested its case, in my mind the case is over." This is consistent with studies showing that "the vast majority of jurors reach a fairly definite decision before all the evidence has been presented in the trial."[19]

The net result is that both oral and written instructions were, as a juror observed, "a formality that you have to go through with." Hence, in *Cleve. v. CEI* the rules of law were ignored by a majority of the jury who relied on their interpretation of primary facts as filtered through preconceived notions of competition.

Moreover, while the minority did refer to the instructions it was not for substantive rules but instead for guidance in the procedural areas of preponderance of the evidence and credibility of witnesses. Thus, these jurors, like the majority, had made up their minds earlier but were more cautious and wanted external support.

5. Summary

Both juries exhibited at least an adequate grasp of primary facts. Jury II was generally, and specifically on technology, more knowledgeable. Moreover, Jury II did not have weak spots whereas Jury I had at best one member who had difficulty understanding the technology of interconnection.

All jurors (and alternates) had difficulty comprehending economic facts. Jury I's comprehension level was low to nonexistent on economic facts and zero as to legal rules from the instructions. They addressed the five special interrogatories without understanding the operative terms or the relevant economic facts. They were guided by "who is right."

While Jury II was more confident about its knowledge of economic facts, its comprehension level was low. The jurors tended to subsume primary facts under a self-defined version of competition. To a majority, the rules of law embodied in the instructions were irrelevant. A minority used the procedural rules from instructions to rationalize a verdict for the defendant.

Static in the Fact-finding Process

1. *The Credibility of Posterior Judgment on Complexity*

It is possible to conclude that neither Jury I nor Jury II understood economic facts in sufficient depth to reach a rational verdict. This does not necessarily mean that Jury II was wrong but only that they were unable to comprehend facts that would be relevant to a rational decision. (Jury I, of course, did not render a verdict.) Likewise, Jury I did not remember and/or understand the final oral instructions, while a majority of Jury II largely ignored written instructions and the minority selectively used self-serving passages. It has also been demonstrated through readability and psycholinguistic studies that the educational level of neither jury was commensurate with the level necessary to comprehend the instructions. Moreover, both trials were long, introducing a fatigue factor; Trial I consumed thirty trial days, lasting over two months, while Trial II was twice as long.

Based on these conclusions, the argument could be made that retrospectively, *Cleve.* v. *CEI* satisfies the criteria of complexity; jurors could not resolve the issues on "the basis of a fair and reasonable assessment of the evidence and a fair and measurable application of the relevant legal rules."[20] Trial time was lengthy, and the case was dominated by "conceptual difficulties in the legal issues and the factual predicates to the issues"[21] which were incomprehensible to the jurors.

However, before a judgment on complexity can reliably be made, the possible impact of additional variables must be considered. As this survey suggests, comprehension is not a separate and discrete element but is instead a component of the events that blend into the gestalt of a trial.

2. *Comprehension Affected by Bias*

In a way difficult to measure, comprehension will be affected by a juror's personal beliefs. According to basic jury psychology:

> [T]he moral and ideological biases held by an observer clearly affect how he actually perceives an opinion presented to him. If the divergence between the observer's own and the presented position is small, the opinion is seen

as actual and fair. If it is great, the view is held to be propagandistic and unfair. Where divergence is small, differences in position are underestimated. Where it is great they are exaggerated.[22]

Voir dire is a battle over bias; each side seeks to gain an edge by impaneling jurors predisposed to its cause. "Jury selection is one of the most important functions a trial lawyer can perform; some lawyers assert that by the time the jury has been chosen, the case has been decided."[23] The city had the opportunity to select from a favorable venire in Trial I, the defense got a good venire in Trial II.

The blue collar people on Jury I were hostile toward management and suspicious of big business. The profit-making CEI was big business and was seen in a negative contrast to the consumer-oriented Muny. To them, it was not a clash between two business firms but rather a question of the survival of a public benefactor.

Interviews were characterized by judgments on the personality and demeanor of participants. To Jury I, the city lawyers were "professional," "sincere," and "well organized." Conversely, they expressed enmity towards CEI's lead counsel; he was described as looking "like something out of a coat rack," "bumbling," "too belligerent," "too hard on witnesses," and "once he got the upper hand he would browbeat." He was accused of coaching witnesses by using "more signals than a football coach." Jury I also directed animosity toward CEI witnesses who, as "cocky" and "paid liars," were perceived as being completely without credibility. Conversely, the city's witnesses, especially W.H. and Dr. W., were praised for expertise and skill in rebuffing overly aggressive cross-examination.

Jury II, who had employment experience in making decisions affecting others, was management oriented and tolerant of free and aggressive competition. They contrasted Muny's managerial incompetence with CEI's efficiency. Several jurors noted with approval the testimony of a CEI executive describing the firm's policy of delegating responsibility down the chain of command. They were favorably impressed with the employment longevity of CEI employees called as witnesses. To Jury II, CEI "is a well-run organization." A juror whose husband operated his own business was incensed at Muny's effort to get what she saw as a free ride at CEI's expense. "Why should you blame someone else even though they are in the same business; there wasn't any contract that [CEI] has got to show [Muny] how they become reliable. I'm not going to tell you my secrets...or give you any help."

There was a complete switch in attitudes toward counsel. Jury II voiced strong approval of the defense's aggressive advocacy tactics, particularly the cross-examinations. They were disdainful, if not contemptuous, of the city's witnesses; Dr. W. was "a little child...if he didn't get his way, he was going to cry." Jury II made withering comments about the city's lawyers, noting what was perceived as their inability to handle witnesses and the judge. They accused them of using the trial as a "learning class." The credibility of the city's lawyers dropped further when the jurors observed one of them writing a letter to his mother while a colleague was questioning a witness. This event was remembered with great amusement as the Dear Mom Incident.

Jury II detected an evolving sense of frustration among city lawyers. Several jurors saw one of the city's team crying in the hallway after a difficult session with Dr. W. and adverse rulings by the court. The overall impression created among the jury was one of defeat; the city lawyers "looked like they were going downhill. They looked their best in the beginning and just kind of went down. Wherein, they [the defense] were getting started...." Another juror said, "I know from watching his [city's lead counsel] facial expressions and...Judge Krupansky told us to take all of that into consideration...I think in watching Mr. N.—I brought this out in the deliberations and some of them [jurors] didn't feel like I did and some of them did, but I think that toward the last couple of weeks before it was finished, I think he was concerned...if he had gotten it across in us."

In summary, personal beliefs favorable to CEI's defense were manifest in the tendency of the interview dialogue to be dominated by value judgments on political interference in business, the obligation to help less efficient rivals, and the personalities of the participants. While jurors can be expected to favor the arguments and lawyers associated with the winning side,[24] the vehemence and the preoccupation with such matters suggested that the case had touched sensitive nerves. In *Cleve. v. CEI* it was ideology that flushed out the bias. It was a classic struggle between antagonistic opposites; populism versus private risk-taking, public ownership versus investor ownership, and consumer versus management. One juror favored CEI so strongly that she wondered why CEI didn't sue Muny.

3. *Distinguishing Bias from Comprehension*

Jurors cope with unwelcome information by ignoring it, distorting it to fit existing values, or minimizing its importance.[25] The extent to which jurors exercised these coping mechanisms to handle information contradicting their beliefs is difficult to fathom. Interviews suggest that Jury I ignored or minimized the importance of CEI witnesses. On the other hand, testimony describing alleged CEI behavior toward Muny touched a sensitive ideological nerve, and became the prop for negative feelings. Rationalization to bring testimony into line with personal values was evident, particularly in the assumption that CEI had a no-strings-attached public responsibility to help Muny.

The values and ideology of Jury II were harmonious with the defendant's position. They screened out information that contradicted their vision of competition. Information that did not fit the management theme was rejected or rationalized. Like Jury I, they strongly identified with the "good guys" and the antagonism toward those associated with the other side confirms the functioning of coping mechanisms.

Thus the problem: How can jury comprehension be measured, much less predicted, when juror perceptions are influenced by pretrial beliefs? The extent of the bias infection is difficult to quantify. For example, how well did the jurors comprehend and retain the testimony of the city's critical witnesses W.H. and Dr. W.? Was the testimony rejected without an effort to comprehend because it came from the "bad guys"? Likewise, what effect did lawyer demeanor have on comprehension—or attentiveness? Perhaps one can at least surmise that the greater the complexity of the material being presented, the greater the chance the juror will tune out if it controverts a bias. Perhaps the extreme example of this is the Trial I juror who expressed resentment at CEI for even raising the natural monopoly defense.

4. The Court's Influence on the Jury

> Although he does not accompany the triers of fact into the jury room to deliberate upon the verdict with them, his every word and look and intonation will, in the course of the trial, weigh with the twelve men as much as, if not more than, his final charge. He has often been described as a thirteenth juror....
>
> —Lloyd Paul Stryker
> *The Art of Advocacy* 32 (1954).

The possible influence that a judge may exert over a jury is acknowledged; according to the Supreme Court, a judge's "lightest words or intonation is received with deference, and may prove controlling."[26] The private views of a judge can be expressed in instructions, comments on evidence and witnesses, and by chastising counsel. Nonverbal cues, such as smiles and gesticulations, may also influence jurors.[27] Judge Krupansky's courtroom personality invites scrutiny for possible impact on comprehension.

Judge Krupansky has the reputation of being a demanding trial judge who maintains a disciplined courtroom. He has been described as "Bullet Bob for this oppressive behavior."[28] Another view is that he is the "most efficient but demanding judge in America."[29] Many lawyers speak approvingly of his ability to maintain control of the affairs of a case. Shortly after the verdict in *Cleve. v. CEI* he was elevated to the Sixth Circuit Court of Appeals.

There were ancillary factors in *Cleve. v. CEI* that increased the problems of supervising a major case. The litigants were long-time bitter rivals, both in the marketplace and in court. As a case with political ramifications, it attracted daily media coverage. Within the courtroom, relations among the participants were strained. Approximately six months prior to Trial I, city lawyers filed a Motion for Disqualification of Judge Krupansky. The motion complained that the "attitude, rulings and other opinions of Honorable Robert B. Krupansky [manifest] a steadfast appearance of a lack of impartiality on his part toward the City."[30]

In addition, the normal adversarial tensions between opposing counsel were exacerbated by the city's motion to disqualify the firm of Squire, Sanders and Dempsey, CEI's counsel, for allegedly using knowledge acquired as the city's bond counsel to the detriment of the city in the antitrust litigation.[31] Both motions were denied, leaving a residue of estrangement among everyone.

After comparing Trial I to combat, a newspaper reporter wrote:

> Krupansky, the one-time B-29 bomber pilot, presided over a battlefield in which the opponents were as bitter toward one another as opposing armies. And, the judge did not always sit on the mount above the fracas.
>
> Although opposing counsel never came to blows, there were after-court swearing incidents. And there was plenty of verbal violence at the bench.[32]

Judge Krupansky conducts litigation according to his Rules of Courtroom Procedure. One rule had an important impact on both trials; when counsel desires to make an objection, counsel must "rise and simply state objection."[33] The reason for the objection is to be given at the judge's bench beyond the hearing of the jury. As a result, when an objection was made, a bench conference of three or four lawyers, a court stenographer and a clerk crowded around the judge. Either from curiosity in what was being said or interest in the ruling on the objection, bench conferences became the fulcrum for the jurors' perception of Judge Krupansky and the lawyers.

Despite hearing only portions of the bench conference commentary, Jury I nevertheless formed definite impressions. The foreman, who was sitting closest to the bench, concluded that the judge "was really picking" on the city's lawyers. She observed that the defense "always won" its objections, adding that "we would talk about that and a lot of jurors felt that the judge was biased...." She also formed the impression that the judge was excessively hard on the city's female litigator; "that girl has got a lot of guts to get up there...as much as he yelled at her, she's got a lot of guts, and we really did think that he picked on her." An alternate complained that the judge was "too hard" on Dr. W., which she considered to be "in very bad taste."

The perception that Judge Krupansky was biased, combined with CEI's aggressive advocacy tactics created an underdog image for the city—an image consistent with the David versus Goliath theme that the city lawyers sought to convey. An influential juror verbalized the significance of the underdog sympathy effect by stating that the judge's treatment of the city gave "you a feeling of—they need some help."

Members of both juries acknowledged that bench conferences interfered with concentration. The Jury I foreman complained that "we thought it was really outrageous as many times as they went up there...." A Jury II alternate was equally irate: "You would sit there half the damn morning and look at the hind end of those attorneys. It just got boring as hell."

As a result of the defendant's change in advocacy tactics, the number and length of bench conferences increased dramatically in Trial II. "As has become routine in this retrial," a news report observed, "bench conferences regularly interrupted the testimony."[34] The vigor and tone of the bench conference dialogue also increased, making it possible for Jury II to hear much of Judge Krupansky's commentary on lawyers and witnesses.

Many jurors heard the judge express irritation with the city's principal witnesses, W.H. and Dr. W. One juror noted that he would roll his eyes during their testimony. The foreman heard the court advise the lawyers "how to deal with W.: 'Don't let him ramble, because that is where they get in trouble'." Several jurors reported that they heard the court threaten to remove the city's first chair from the proceeding. "I heard...the judge tell N. that if he didn't start getting his act together, he would get another lawyer."[35] The jurors agreed with the foreman that the defense's success in rulings on objections and the court's criticism reflected badly on the city's lawyers and its case. According to one juror:

> [A] lot of times where the lawyer was constantly not laying a proper foundation and then [CEI's counsel] would object and they would approach the bench and the judge would just tell them, "If you are not going to lay the proper foundation, you are not to continue this line of questioning" and he said that many times and probably most of the time was to [the city's first chair] and if the man is as good as they say he is and he is the city's top lawyer, I felt that was a poor excuse of the reputation of the city having lawyers that are supposed to be professional and know what they are doing and he is not a young man. I mean he is not old, so he should be experienced, he should know how to lay a proper foundation and after a while I would say lay a proper foundation before it was ever objected to, because he was misleading, he wasn't doing it right. I just felt he wasn't good.
>
> QUESTION: And that made an impression on you?
>
> ANSWER: Yes. It did. He is supposed to know his job better than that. He got called on too many times.

The foreman concluded: "I heard these things that to me just proved that the city did not prepare itself with the tons of paper it had...that they had a poor case."

Static in the Fact-finding Process 93

5. Reaching a Verdict before Deliberation

Jurors with strong personal beliefs are likely to make up their minds before deliberation. Based upon empirical experience, Vinson says:

> The most important thing learned about the decision-making process is that many jurors come to a decision very early in the trial and thus seek support for their conclusions.... It was clear that many jurors defend retrospectively decisions already made. This phenomenon continues to be seen in all subsequent jury research.... Jurors do not come into the courtroom with a *tabula rasa*. They use their values, beliefs, attitudes, and past experiences to reach a decision almost at once.[36]

Body language and the demeanor of Jury II gave the clear impression that they had made up their minds long before they began deliberation.[37] It is likely that many jurors began to favor the defendant as a result of the cross-examination of W.H. This occurred early in the trial, on the afternoon of the eighth day. My diary of trial observation reveals the jury's growing disdain for H: "Vigorous cross-examination of H." "Gloves are off between L. (CEI counsel) and H." "Number 4 watching H. very intently." "Number 1 smiling at Numbers 9 and 10." "I don't think that the jury is buying H.'s story—successful impeachment?" "H. getting evasive." "Numbers 1 and 3 amused when H. got caught and had to agree with L. over interpretation." "H. is on the ropes." "Number 1 and 7 grinning at H.'s effort to avoid agreeing with L." "Bench conference—L. [said]: 'He's telling me something different.' Jury heard his comment." "Number 1 has a big grin—also Number 3." "Number 12 amused, grinned at audience at L.'s outburst." "H. chastised by Krupansky." "Number 4 appears irritated at H." "They don't like him." "The judge comments: 'Respond to the question'." "Number 1 looking to audience and shaking his head."

Interviews confirmed that the cross-examination of H. was a significant influence and that his testimony on mismanagement critically affected the credibility of the city's case. According to an alternate, after H. testified, "we thought the trial was over." She indicated that she would have voted against the city regardless of what the instructions said. The foreman summed up: "Once the city rested its case... in my mind, the case is over. They could have... stopped the trial because they didn't have to go any further." Other jurors agreed. An alternate revealed that she made up her mind to vote for the city three quarters through the city's case. But perhaps the most obvious indication that Jury II had made up its mind is the short length of deliberation—approximately five hours. The quick decision did not surprise an alternate, who detected that the jurors "leaned all the way toward CEI... especially toward the last."

Jury I exhibited very little animation during the course of the trial and thus was hard to read from observation. Nonetheless, based on their deep antagonism toward everyone associated with the defendant and the rationalization with CEI's perceived violation of a duty to serve the public, one can surmise a predeliberation conclusion by the majority. To the dissenter, the majority "already had made up their minds that it [CEI] was guilty down the line."

The probable consequence of an early commitment by a juror is the reduction of interest and concentration. To the extent that interest is maintained, the juror is likely to focus on testimony that supports and rationalizes the decision. It is reasonable to surmise that the ultimate impact on comprehension is negative.

6. The Unanticipated

Despite careful planning and sustained efforts to control the script, it is impossible to anticipate incidents that may influence a jury. For example, Jury II formed a negative view of the Dear Mom Incident. Observation of one of the city lawyers crying in the hallway was seen as a sign of inexperience and a disintegrating case. Several jurors drove by the Municipal Light plant each day to jury duty and thus, according to their perceptions, got a daily reminder of its disrepair and Muny's mismanagement. Perhaps the most provocative incident was when a juror observed the city's chief economic expert as he faced a coat rack in the hallway outside the courtroom:

> Dr. W. is standing there looking at them coat hangers and he hit the first one and the first one hit the second one and the third and the fourth, you know, chain reaction and...he would wait for a while and then he would do it again...bing, bing, bing. Then he did it again. And, he was just sitting there staring at them coat racks bump into each other and we're looking at him and I couldn't believe it. I said, my gosh, I wonder how much they are paying this guy for playing with all the coat racks.... He did it about four or five times and then he would just stare at them for a while and walked off.... It was strange, it was really strange.... Maybe he was trying to think of the economics.

Is Reliable Prediction of Complexity Possible?

1. Comprehension

Granting a motion to strike a jury on the basis of complexity assumes that the court can make a reliable prediction of the jury's capacity to comprehend. The courts have relied on three indicators: duration or length of trial, difficulty in understanding facts, and the conceptual difficulty of substantive issues.

The survey confirms the utility of these indicators in furnishing insights into jury comprehension. A protracted trial is likely to interfere with retention and as the volume of exhibits and testimony increases, comprehension levels will drop. By classifying facts according to subject, it was possible to identify varying levels of comprehension. All the jurors seemed to have enough understanding of historical and technological facts to make a rational judgment. Conversely, none of the jurors had a grasp of economic facts at a level sufficient to evaluate the competing arguments. Since the instructions played a peripheral role in the case, it was difficult to ascertain juror comprehension. The oral presentation was virtually useless to Jury I, while Jury II, with the exception of several members focusing on rationalization activators, relied on perceptions formed during the trial. Nevertheless, psycholinguistic experiments and readability studies indicate a high level of conceptual difficulty for the substantive issues described in the *Cleve. v. CEI* instructions.

These observations are subject to an important qualification: as part of the gestalt of a trial, comprehension is affected by other factors. For example, the pretrial beliefs of a juror can affect the way information is perceived. Information may be rejected, distorted, or exaggerated. Concentration levels will subside when testimony contradicts a juror's values. The more complicated the negative information, the less the juror's tolerance. Where strong beliefs exist, as is likely in antitrust, jurors will form judgments during the trial and, as likely occurred in *Cleve. v. CEI*, "pick the winner" long before deliberation. Under these conditions, jurors "turn off" to negative testimony and hence efforts to measure comprehension become difficult or futile.

Although it is difficult to measure the extent of influence, it is clear that personal beliefs affected comprehension in *Cleve. v. CEI.* Both juries expressed strong views on the proper scope of competition in the electrical utility industry. The populist instincts of Jury I surfaced in their perceptions of the defendant's witnesses and lawyers and their interpretation of evidence. Jury II was at the other end of the ideological spectrum, and the interviews left no doubt that a commitment to vigorous competition, efficiency, and dislike of political interference in business influenced the way they digested testimony.

2. Antitrust and Ideology

Perhaps the most significant finding of the survey is that the personal belief most frequently expressed and exerting the greatest influence on perception was ideology. The survey thus exposed another factor that bears on comprehension and complexity: antitrust is ideological and jurors have an ideological stake in the outcome of litigation.

Antitrust is subsumed under the ideology of free enterprise. Free enterprise, also known as capitalism or the competitive system, is the method the political system has adopted for allocating resources. The Sherman Act, enacted in 1890, was an effort to establish general principles to maintain a political ideal. It is "an expression of a social philosophy, an educative force, and a political symbol of extraordinary potency."[38] The language of the statutes is flexible and, according to the Supreme Court, possesses a "generality and adaptability comparable to that found to be desirable in constitutional provisions."[39] Under these conditions, it was inevitable that antitrust would become an ideological battleground.

There has been persistent and violent controversy over the proper function of antitrust. The populist philosophy advocates the use of antitrust to preserve or impose the Jeffersonian ideals of a pluralistic economy.[40] This clashes with the traditional view that the antitrust laws are neutral and become operative only when competition, as distinguished from competitors, is harmed.[41] The new trend exalts efficiency and economies.[42]

On the other hand, reformers argue that antitrust should correct sociopolitical ills such as racial discrimination, dehumanizing assembly lines, and pollution.[43] The most recent controversy concerns the use of economics. Now firmly entrenched as the centerpiece of antitrust, the debate centers on the appropriate set of principles to apply. While economists are more contentious than lawyers they operate with a significant advantage; they can utilize the liturgy of mathematical equation and economic model to propagandize value judgments. Academics, frustrated with the whimsical meanderings of appellate opinions and searching for a holy grail in antitrust policy, enthusiastically embraced what was perceived as symmetry and certainty in economics.[44] With persistent cacophony, various factions compete for control of the antitrust dialogue.[45]

The decisions mirror the twists and turns of the debates. Sprinkled with buzz words, the cases are enigmatic, confusing, and contradictory. Workable competition competes with pure competition, equal opportunity access to the marketplace clashes with efficiency, and bigness is confronted by *mom-and-popism*. The classic example of convolution is the *Alcoa*[46] opinion, which remains the primary authority for monopolization—the violation alleged in *Cleve. v. CEI*. Leaving a legacy of puzzlement, Judge Hand condemned monopoly, exonerated it if the result of "superior skill, foresight, and industry," but then condemned success due to experience, trade connection, or elite management. Not finished, Hand threw in some ideological gems by saying that antitrust should be used to "perpetuate and preserve, for its own sake and in spite of possible costs, an organization of industry in small units which can effectively compete with each other."[47] Judge Wyzanski described the scene at the trial court level:

> A District Judge knows that he cannot give any authoritative reconciliation of opinions rendered by appellate courts. And in connection with the Sherman Act, it is delusive to treat opinions written by different judges at different times as pieces of a jigsaw puzzle which can be, by effort, fitted correctly into a single pattern.[48]

3. *Ideology, Comprehension, and the Jury*

Antitrust burdens the legal system with material that challenges the comprehension of sophisticated judges and lawyers, while inspiring turgid prose by scholars. Due to the intrinsic composition of violations like monopolization, antitrust is complex. Hence the credible argument that, by definition, antitrust is *a priori* conceptually difficult, thereby satisfying the Third Circuit's third indicium of complexity.[49]

A fertile source of complexity is ideology. While litigation deals with subissues like relevant market and exclusionary conduct, the overriding concern is the ideology of competition.

The chorus of the interviews was the perception by all jurors that *Cleve. v. CEI* was a contest over how the marketplace should function. The jurors evaluated evidence in terms of what they expected from competition. There was an obvious and clear-cut ideological difference between Jury I and Jury II. The first jury assumed a populist form of competition as the ideal; where electricity is involved, the consumer is best served by cooperation rather than hard competition. Moreover, the government is a legitimate provider of power, even if tax-subsidized. Jury II was at the other end of the spectrum. They were adamant that it is inappropriate for government to compete with private enterprise and scornful of the wastes they associated with a municipally operated facility.

There are two additional ramifications from antitrust as a form of ideological litigation. First, when the ideological content of a trial is high, comprehension is likely to be affected. Jurors tend to focus and concentrate on those factors that are supported by, or support, their ideological bias. Since the emotional commitment to ideology is high, the bias influence will be strong. Information that contradicts or is inconsistent with ideology will be ignored.

Secondly, based on the ideological character of antitrust, a policy argument can be made against *a priori* striking a jury. The function of a jury in antitrust is to express ideology by interpreting the statutes in a way that reflects ideals of competition perceived as consistent with the prevailing mood. Where competing ideologies exist, each is entitled to be heard, and neither the populist view of Jury I nor the laissez faire view of Jury II is correct or incorrect. In urging caution in dispensing with jury trials, Professor Lempert observes:

> Finally it must be recognized that complex cases—such as large-scale antitrust litigation—are some of the most "political" cases that the system hears. Vast sums of money are involved, and the structure of the nation's largest companies may be at issue. The power of business vis-à-vis consumers is inescapably implicated. Even if the litigation is so complicated that the jurors have no popular view of where justice lies (apart from the legal test) and no understanding of the political implications of different decisions, judges may well have such a view and such understanding. Unlike most jurors, judges have often been either personally involved in politics or experienced in representing clients before political bodies. In recent years, moreover, a number of judges have received formal training in economics—at no personal expense—from an institute that reportedly takes a decidedly partisan view of the kinds of economic policy questions that are commonly implicated in complex litigation. In short, judges will have a good idea of the consequences that different verdicts entail, and they may strongly prefer one outcome to another. If the jury does not infuse popular morality into cases that are so complex as to defy the layperson's sense of the moral, it may play the equally important role—and one also contemplated by the framers—of preventing judgments in such important cases from being dominated by the morality of an elite.[50]

Conclusions and Recommendations

The jurors and alternates who served in *Cleve. v. CEI* did have serious problems in comprehending vital information. At the same time, the survey fails to support the assumption followed by the Third Circuit that complex litigation can be *a priori* identified. While the indicia used by the courts supply useful insights, they do not take into account the effects of the various forms of static discussed in previous sections. Likewise, the difficulty in separating comprehension factors from static renders *posterior* judgments unreliable.

The ideological character of antitrust further complicates the problem. Measuring comprehension is a nebulous task at best when value judgments on competition are involved. At this point Professor Lempert's argument becomes persuasive and it is preferable to allow the jury to make the choice between value judgments.

The bottom line question is whether evaluative techniques can be devised to segregate comprehension, thereby enabling accurate prediction. Based on the experience of this survey, the answer is no. Utilization of an extensive range of methods while collecting and evaluating data over a two-year period teaches that the greater the depth and thoroughness of the research, the greater the level of static uncovered. Moreover, even if reliable techniques were available, courts do not have the time, the expertise, and the resources to apply them to trial litigation.

The survey does not justify—nor endorse—the status quo. The challenge is to create conditions that improve the opportunity for comprehension and filter out the interference of static.

1. Trial Management

Over the past decade the bench and bar have expended considerable time on improving trial management. The Manual for Complex Litigation contains recommendations for improving efficiency and reducing the time between filing the complaint and termination. Antitrust received special attention from the National Commission for the Review of Antitrust Laws and Procedures, which suggested ways to expedite complex cases.[51] The thrust of the various studies and guides is on improving trial management procedures—not jury comprehension. Nevertheless, to the extent that the changes reduce repetition and speed up the process, they make positive contributions to jury retention and comprehension.

A major trial management problem is coping with the avalanche of documentary evidence. While document control is primarily a management burden for court and counsel, it is also a significant source of static in comprehension. Jurors and alternates complained about the number of exhibits, the inability to keep up with them, and the failure of the court or counsel to distinguish the important from the irrelevant. Some typical comments from Jury II: "Didn't try to keep up [with exhibits]"; "Most were a waste"; "I relied on the testimony"; "Exhibits too technical—didn't do much for me."

The obvious remedy is for the court to impose one of the standard recommendations and require counsel to economize on documentary evidence. As a responsibility of the court, document control varies from court to court.[52] While the court is under the duty to exercise management skills,[53] ultimately the burden falls on counsel, who might be more likely to economize on their own initiative if they fully appreciated the negative effects of inefficient document management on comprehension. Counsel should also comprehend that unless the jury hears otherwise, all documents are equal and become part of the blur of exhibits. Hence, critical documents should be distinguished. Moreover, jurors should be supplied with an ongoing index containing brief descriptions of the exhibits.[54] Document retrieval during deliberation—which jurors complained as being difficult, if not impossible—should be systematized and keyed to the exhibits.

2. Creating an Educational Atmosphere

Originally selected for their familiarity with the parties and facts of the case,[55] jurors are now carefully screened to eliminate those who know too much about the conflict. They are impaneled for their ignorance of the case, do not know each other, and are called upon to grasp material that teams of lawyers and experts have taken years to organize and assimilate. The lawyers, judge, and experts speak an esoteric and mysterious language in front of a passive audience. As an audience, jurors are second class citizens—they cannot boo, applaud, ask questions, or even discuss the drama among themselves. The system demands comprehension but purposely erects barriers that contradict basic educational principles. The situation demands attitudinal and procedural changes.

a. Attitudinal Changes

The psychology of the adversarial system must be revised. Trials are dominated by the personalities of the lawyers. Trial lawyers are by self-selection and training egocentric; they see the trial as a fight with a winner and a loser, the latter being anathema. As Francis Wellman observed, "The advocates gradually become the principal actors in the drama, much as if they were playing leading roles on the stage."[56] Opposing experts are neutralized by various ploys, most of which are designed to create static between them and the jury. The objective is persuasion, not education. "The most important of all trial techniques is to be persuasive."[57]

The traditional advocacy mentality is inconsistent with comprehension. Trial lawyers in antitrust litigation must first accept the necessity of replacing the adversarial priority with the educational objective, and, secondly, must adopt procedures that bring the jury into the trial as active participants in education.

b. Jury Orientation

Upon being impaneled, the jury should receive a thorough orientation. They should be given an education in the characteristics of the adversarial system and their role as fact-finders, and a description of what is expected of them once they begin deliberation. Emphasis should be given to explaining the objective of instructions and special interrogatories. This would prevent the experience of the *Cleve. v. CEI* jurors, who went into deliberation assuming their sole function was to determine guilt or innocence and that the judge would calculate damages.

A disorganized and confused deliberation process interferes with the open and lucid exchange of information and thus inhibits knowledgeable jurors from educating their colleagues. These conditions can contribute to hostilities which can, as occurred with Jury I, ultimately terminate the process in a hung jury. To prevent this, jurors should receive (either orally or in literature) a thorough orientation in deliberation procedures. The most important point is to provide them with procedural suggestions: how to elect a foreman, the possible advantages of electing a secretary, ideas for arranging a discussion format and voting procedures.[58] Ideally, this information should be imparted at the initial orientation and again when the jury begins deliberation. It would eliminate the mystery and confusion that troubled the jurors—especially Jury I.

Preliminary instructions can make a contribution but only if coverage is restricted to procedural and evidentiary definitions such as burden of proof, preponderance of evidence, and credibility. Any additional information conveyed through preliminary instructions will be lost and could interfere with comprehension and the evidentiary material. Preliminary instructions should encourage the jury to perform its assigned task: digest the facts.

The most important part of orientation is to integrate the jury into the fabric of the trial. The court and lawyers should combine to make a presentation of an overview of the trial; the identity and history of the parties and the industry, and a description by the court of the allegations. If technology or other complex information is involved, the court should consider the use of a court appointed expert for lecture purposes. The details of the presentation should be carefully worked out under the supervision of the court with the objective of creating an educational atmosphere. Given the lecture format, it should not be difficult to sift out bias from the presentation.

During orientation, the first exhibit is introduced—a flow chart compiled under court supervision of what is going to happen, the order of appearance and names of witnesses, brief descriptions of exhibits, with all information keyed to the allegations. The flow chart should be large and visually available to the jury throughout the trial. As they occur, changes can be recorded on the chart.

Accompanying the flow chart is a glossary of terms made available to jurors. By defining terms and describing the cast of characters in the drama, the glossary embellishes the effectiveness of the chart.

a. Two-way Communication

The most effective way to establish a learning environment is to permit two-way communication. As a legacy of the lawyers' dominance of the trial dialogue, trials are conducted according to a *linear-one-way* communication process in which information is transmitted to the jurors without allowing them to respond. "It is bizarre," says a critic, "that those people who have to decide the issues of the trial are not permitted...to ask questions."[59]

Research reveals that linear-one-way communication distorts reception in numerous ways: information is ignored which does not conform to the perceived stereotype of the communicator; the receiver stresses details that are within the familiar pattern of the stereotype, and the message is condensed into easily remembered packages with unfamiliar terms being excluded. Significant to jury comprehension, the longer and the greater the complexity of the linear-one-way communication, the greater the level of inaccuracies in reception. In addition, the receiver's hostility and frustration increase.[60]

Circular or two-way communication, that is, allowing jurors to ask questions throughout the trial (including orientation), will improve the accuracy of the transmission.[61] Jurors will gain confidence from two-way participation with a concomitant jump in interest and concentration. The very act of asking a question involves analysis and self-education. It puts pressure on the lawyers to improve communication skills and stress education rather than persuasion. To the advantage of everyone, questions

Conclusions and Recommendations 103

will identify comprehension problem areas and give the lawyers an opportunity to correct misapprehensions.

The benefits far outweigh the disadvantages.[62] While the trial may be lengthened, this is a modest price to pay for better comprehension in an already long trial. There is the danger that a question will violate evidentiary rules and thereby put counsel in the dilemma of objecting in the presence of the jury. This can be avoided by having written questions channeled to the judge, who can rule on objections at the bench. Thus if there is a "heavy," it is the judge.

d. Note-taking

Precluding jurors from taking notes is another litigation antique. The custom dates to the time of limited literacy and the concern that notes in the juryroom would unduly influence illiterates.[63] The assumed influence of notes over recollection persists. Additional problems are cited: note-taking will favor the superfluous over the relevant, jurors will take inaccurate notes and miss observing the demeanor of witnesses.[64]

Courts are beginning to use their discretion to permit note-taking.[65] Literacy levels have improved so there is no reason to assume that jurors will be awed by notes. This was confirmed by the survey, which revealed a nonchalant attitude and split on the possible contribution of notes. Some jurors did keep a list of witnesses, which they found helpful. The prevailing attitude was that note-taking was a matter of preference; it would have provided help to the juror, but notes would not have unduly influenced those who relied on recollection.

The other criticisms are rooted in surmise, and one can argue that the dedication to concentration necessary for note-taking will improve attention and recognition of relevant testimony, thereby elevating comprehension levels. Perhaps of equal importance, note-taking provides a psychological boost by getting the juror more involved in the process.[66]

e. Interaction

At lunch breaks and the conclusion of the day, the court delivered the standard charge admonishing the jury not to discuss the case among themselves or with others. This achieved the highest memory rating by both juries. The restriction on intragroup discussion should be terminated so that jurors can discuss the details of the trial as it unfolds. Group discussion is a logical adjunct to note-taking and two-way communication.

The rationale for the restriction is that jurors should keep an open mind until deliberation and exchanging views will lead to an early decision.

> The theory of our system is that the conclusions to be reached in a case will be induced only by evidence and argument in open court, and not by any outside influence, whether of private talk or public print.[67]

It is also assumed that a jury may be vulnerable to the influence of an assertive or dominant juror. These arguments do not survive examination. Research, including this survey, indicates that regardless of the admonishment, jurors are likely to form early predeliberation judgments. Moreover, it is just as logical to assume that group discussion will dilute the vigor of a dominant juror. However, the strongest argument against the restriction is that it has a negative impact on comprehension.

Advocates of the jury system cite the benefits of the interaction effect; the collective knowledge of the jury as a group exceeds the knowledge of individual jurors.[68] Interaction under existing conditions is expected to suddenly blossom after the evidence is in and the jury begins deliberation.[69] The problem is that by this time it is too late for effective interaction, and views have crystallized, rendering advice unwelcome. Moreover, by the time of deliberation, information insights that jurors could have exchanged during the trial are lost to memory lapses.

The restriction has other negative effects: the extent to which jurors adhere to the restriction will vary. My surmise is that jurors did engage in small group "fugitive" conversations. Fugitive conversations are not tested by the collective knowledge of the group, thereby increasing the possibility that incorrect information will influence a juror. Fugitive conversation also fosters the creation of cliques, further exacerbating misinformation problems. When jurors do adhere to the admonishment, conversations converge on safe topics such as the performance of counsel and the personality of witnesses.[70] As the trial drags on, these topics take on an exaggerated importance to become the fulcrum for judgments on factual issues. Thus the dress of lawyers and witnesses and their idiosyncracies become facts.

f. Transcripts and Instructions

Several jurors indicated that access to daily transcripts would have been helpful. This request should be accommodated. This would reinforce memory, encourage concentration, and enhance comprehension.

The court should provide the jury with written instructions. As an experienced federal district judge observed, "Written instructions to the jury are absolutely indispensable."[71] Availability is a waste, however, unless the instructions are written to be understood. The parties should be encouraged to engage in comprehension testing and redrafting.[72] The final instructions, time permitting, should be reviewed by a court-appointed expert.

Final Comments

Relying on a survey of two juries to make assumptions on comprehension is necessarily risky. Nevertheless, some cautious generalizations can be offered. One can conclude with confidence that if a trial exhibits characteristics similar to *Cleve. v. CEI*, the mixture of intangibles will preclude an infallible prediction that the litigation is too complex for the understanding of a jury. Thus the empirical data from this jury survey does not support the underlying assumption of the Third Circuit in *In re Japanese Elect. Prod. Antitrust Lit.*[73] The clear lesson from this study is that a juror's comprehension is the result of a plethora of variables. Pretrial beliefs and attitudes, reacting to the evidence and the personalities of the participants, can enhance or inhibit understanding. Moreover, we know very little about the consequences of personality interaction among jurors who are thrown together for eight or nine hours a day. Each *Cleve. v. CEI* jury, over the course of the trials, evolved to form its own distinctive personality.

The significance of the ideological factor stands out. Antitrust, especially monopolization litigation, is an open invitation to jurors to express their value judgments on competition, conduct, and bigness. Concentration and comprehension are enhanced by testimony that reinforces a juror's ideological predilections. Nonreinforcing evidence is rejected or given little attention.

Jurors begin to make a choice early in the trial as to whom they feel is entitled to the verdict so that by deliberation a decision has been crystallized. The impact on comprehension of a subconscious decision favoring one side is dramatic; jurors will not energize the concentration commitment necessary to understand complex testimony.

Assuming that the jury is able to acquire a solid grasp of the testimony and evidence, they still must acquire knowledge of the law of the trial as given in the instructions. Research, including this survey, convincingly establishes that jurors do not learn from instructions, further isolating them from information needed for a rational decision. If instructions have any utility, it is to provide a source of statements that reinforce ideological beliefs.

Notes

1. In re Japanese Electronic Products Antitrust Litigation, 631 F.2d 1069, 1092 (3rd Cir. 1980).
2. *See* ILC Peripherals Leasing Corp. v. IBM Corp., 458 F. Supp. 423 (N.D. Calif. 1978).
3. Section 0.10–0.23, Manual for Complex Litigation (5th ed. 1982).
4. L. Sullivan, Handbook of the Law of Antitrust Law and Policy 96 (1977).
5. Byars v. Bluff City News Co., 699 F.2d 843, 858 (6th Cir. 1979).
6. Protracted Civil Trials: Views from the Bench and Bar (Fed. Judicial Center 1981).
7. Trial days and trial hours reflect two different, equally important burdens of long trials. For jurors, the number of trial days seems to be the more sensitive measure of burden. Whether the trial day lasts two hours or six hours, the juror loses a full day in terms of his or her ability to work or conduct personal affairs in the usual manner. On the other hand, the number of trial hours more accurately reflects the burden of trial on judicial resources and personnel. A judge can usually move easily between courtroom and chambers; thus, a short trial day permits the judge to work on other judicial business. Protracted Civil Trials, *supra* note 6 at 70.
8. *Trial day* refers to time the jury hears testimony and excludes days the lawyers argued motions before the court.
9. Protracted Civil Trials, *supra* note 6 at 3.
10. *See generally*, J. Frank, Law and the Modern Mind (1930); K. Llewellyn, The Common Law Tradition: Deciding Appeals (1960).
11. *See* Weiner, *The Civil Jury Trial and the Law-Fact Distinction*, 54 Calif. L. Rev. 1867 (1966).
12. In most controversies there are two types of fact questions involved—questions as to evidentiary facts and questions as to ultimate facts. The first involve the raw elements of the case, usually what the witnesses observed by their physical senses—what they saw, heard, and the like. The second have to do with the conclusions to be drawn from the evidentiary facts. Brown, *Fact and Law in Judicial Review*, 56 Harv. L. Rev. 899, 902 (1943).

13. Industrial organization economics, a variant of microeconomics, adheres to the market structure (concentration, product differentiation and barriers to entry)-performance (efficiency and progressiveness) paradigm. The accepted wisdom is that the structure of the market determines conduct and conduct determines performance. *See* J. Bain, Industrial Organization (2d ed. 1968); Industrial Concentration: The New Learning (Goldschmid, Mann, Weston, ed. 1974).
14. Courts have developed shorthand techniques for bridging the gap between facts and liability. Some violations, such as price fixing, are presumed to harm competition and are classified as *per se* illegal. Another method is to rely on the assumptions of economics. See Austin, *A Priori Mechanical Jurisprudence In Antitrust*, 53 Minn. L. Rev. 739 (1969).
15. Att'y. Gen. Nat'l. Comm. Antitrust Rep. 35 (1955).
16. B. Sales, A. Elwork, J. Alfini, *Making Jury Instructions Understandable*, Release, June 1, 1981, Dept. of Justice of the United States (Nat. Institute of Justice). *See* Charrow & Charrow, *Making Legal Language Understandable: A Psycholinguistic Study of Jury Instructions*, 79 Colum. L. Rev. 1306, 1308 n.8 (1979); Schwarzer, *Communicating With Juries: Problems and Remedies*, 69 Calif. L. Rev. 731 (1981); Forston, *Sense and Non-Sense: Jury Trial Communication*, 1975 B.Y.U. L. Rev. 601; Strawn & Buchanan, *Jury Confusion: A Threat to Justice*, Judicature, Vol. 59, no. 10, May 1976, p. 478.
17. Sales, Elwork, Alfini, *Improving Comprehension for Jury Instructions* 23, 69 (B. Sales ed. 1977).
18. Forston, *supra* note 16 at 610.
19. *Id.* at 612.
20. In re Japanese Electronic Products Antitrust Lit., 631 F.2d 1069, 1079 (3d Cir. 1980).
21. *Id.* at 1088.
22. Bevan, Albert, Loiseaux, Mayfield, Wright, *Jury Behavior as a Function of the Prestige of the Foreman and the Nature of his Leadership*, J. Of Public Law 419, 421. *See* Weld & Danzig, *A Study of the Way in Which a Verdict is Reached by a Jury*, 53 Am. J. Psych. 518 (1940).
23. Hunt, *Putting Juries on the Couch*, N.Y. Times Magazine, Nov. 28, 1982, p. 70, 82. *See* Vinson, *Psychological Anchors: Influencing the Jury*, 8 Litigation 20 (1982).
24. Hoffman, Brodley, *Jurors on Trial*, 17 Mo. L. Rev. 235, 242 (1952).
25. Vinson, *supra* note 23.
26. Starr v. U.S., 153 U.S. 614, 626 (1894).
27. Conner, *The Trial Judge, His Facial Expressions, Gestures, and Demeanor—Their Effect on the Administration of Justice*, 9 Trial Law Guide, August 1965, at 61. Note, *Judges' Nonverbal Behavior in Jury Trials: A Threat to Judicial Impartiality*, 61 Va. L. Rev. 1266 (1975).
28. Whelan, *The High and the Mighty*, Cleveland Magazine, May 1980, pp. 53, 54.

29. *Id.*
30. Plaintiff's Motion for Disqualification of Judge Robert B. Krupansky, Feb. 28, 1980, p. 2.
31. City of Cleveland v. CEI Co., 440 F. Supp. 193 (N.D. Ohio 1977), aff'd, 573 F.2d 1310 (1977).
32. Cleveland Press, Jan. 10, 1980, p. A-10.
33. Krupansky, *Courtroom Procedure*, Order No. 9-24-76, Rule E.
34. Cleveland Plain Dealer, Aug. 26, 1981, p. 6-A.
35. I could not find this incident in the transcript of Trial II.
36. Vinson, *The Shadow Jury: An Experiment in Litigation Science*, 68 ABA J. 1243, 1244, Oct. 1982. For additional studies *see* Forston, *Sense and Non-Sense: Jury Trial Communication*, 1975 B.Y.U. L. Rev. 601, 612 n.24.
37. The reporter who covered the trial on a daily basis wrote:

> With a certitude that defies comprehension, jurors in the retrial of Cleveland's antitrust suit against Cleveland Electric Illuminating Co. found quickly and apparently easily in favor of CEI.
> The blur of witnesses and information thrown at them over 63 days makes it hard to understand how they could come back with their decision convinced and sure.
> One theory speaks to the issue. It is that a jury decides rather early in the process and then continues to look for things that sustain its convictions.
> Thus, when jurors decided in CEI's favor, it helped them along when Harold H. Wein, the city's economics witness, admitted he made a $4 million mistake in his calculation of the damages.
> It helped when Warren D. Hinchee, the former commissioner of the Municipal Light Plant, hedged and slipped on questions from the often incredulous CEI lawyer John Lansdale.
> It helped when Lansdale, in exasperation, repeatedly said, "Oh, Mr. Hinchee," the words dogging Hinchee's credibility.
> It helped when city lawyers were constantly interrupted by Lansdale, chopping off the flow of questions and answers and disrupting understanding.

Cleveland Plain Dealer, Oct. 11, 1981, p. A-25.
38. Bork, Bowman, *The Crisis in Antitrust*, 65 Colum. L. Rev. 363 (1965).
39. Sugar Institute, Inc. v. U.S., 297 U.S. 553, 600 (1936).
40. Austin, *The Emergence of Societal Antitrust*, 47 N.Y.U. L. Rev. 903 (1972).
41. C. Kaysen, D. Turner, Antitrust Policy: An Economic and Legal Analysis (1965).
42. R. Bork, The Antitrust Paradox (1978).
43. Austin, *supra* note 40. There are those who argue that antitrust is an establishment instrument, *see* Phillips, *Antitrust Policies: Could They Be Tools of the Establishment?*, in Antitrust Policy and Economic Welfare 54 (W. Sichel, ed. 1970); that it is counterproductive, *see* J. Galbraith, American Capitalism, Chp. V (1952); or superfluous, *see* Hofstadter, *What Happened to the Antitrust Movement?*, in The Business Establishment 113 (E. Cheit, ed. 1964).
44. *See* Leff, *Economic Analysis of Law: Some Realism About Nominalism*, 60 Va. L. Rev. 451 (1974).

45. Posner describes the problem:

> If it is desirable and proper that antitrust policy rest on a point of economic theory... then it is reasonable to turn to the economics profession for guidance in reaching the general goal to a set of usable guidelines. Unfortunately, the profession is deeply divided on the critical issues. Virtually every initiative that the Antitrust Division has taken, or would take, has had or would have its defenders among reputable economists. The Assistant Attorney General in charge of Antitrust will rarely be competent to evaluate competing schools of economic thought, and, if he is, he is likely to have his own *parti pris*.

Posner, *A Program for the Antitrust Division*, 38 U. Chicago L. Rev. 500, 506-7 (1971).

46. U.S. v. Aluminum Co. of America, 148 F.2d 416 (2d Cir. 1945).

47. *Id.* at 429.

48. U.S. v. United Shoe Mach. Corp., 110 F. Supp. 295, 342 (D. Mass. 1953), *aff'd per curiam*, 347 U.S. 521 (1954).

49. In re Japanese Electronic Prod. Antitrust Lit., 631 F.2d 1069 (3d Cir. 1980).

50. Lempert, *Civil Juries and Complex Cases: Let's Not Rush to Judgment*, 80 Mich. L. Rev. 68, 84 (1981). *See* Kirst, *The Jury's Historic Domain In Complex Cases*, 58 Wash. L. Rev. 1 (1982).

51. *See also*, Expediting Pretrials and Trials of Antitrust Cases, ABA Antitrust Section, Monograph 3.

52. "[A] special committee appointed by Judge Eagleson to study the protracted civil trial phenomenon in Los Angeles found that the reasons for long trials may have more to do with local procedure and the lack of a strong judicial hand than with novel legal issues. The causes... included repetitive questioning in multi-party cases, use and abuse of expert witnesses, cumulative evidence and lawyers who 'won't agree to the obvious'." Granelli, *Long Trials Play Havoc With Courts*, Nat. L.J., Dec. 27, 1982.

53. "The trial judge has the undoubted power and inescapable duty to control the processing of a case from the time it is filed." Section 1.10, Manual for Complex Litigation (5th ed. 1981).

54. *See* Grady, *Trial Management and Jury Control In Antitrust Cases*, 51 Antitrust L.J. 249, 253 (1982).

55. Schwarzer, *supra* note 16 at 732.

56. F. Wellman, Gentlemen of the Jury 93 (1924).

57. Glickman, *Persuasion in Litigation*, 8 Litigation 30 (1982).

58. *See* G. Lehman, What You Need to Know for Jury Duty.

59. Swartz, *New Voice For Jurors Is Proposed*, Nat. L.J., Nov. 16, 1981, pp. 3, 38.

60. Forston, *supra* note 16 at 628-29.

61. "Experiments have demonstrated with consistency that the accuracy of

information transferred by two-way communcation far exceeds the accuracy of information passed by one-way communication." Forston, *supra* note 16 at 629.

62. See Forston, *supra* note 16 at 630-31; Ranii, *Judges Push Increased Jury Role*, Nat. L.J., Aug. 16, 1982, p. 1; Swartz, *supra* note 59; Strawn, Munsterman, *Helping Juries Understand Complex Cases*, Judicature, Vol. 65, No. 8-9, March-April 1982, p. 444. See Lempert, *Was Data General Case Too Much for Jury to Handle?*, Legal Times of Wash., March 15, 1982, p. 39, for a discussion of juror questioning in an antitrust case. Plaintiff lawyers, who won, praised the jury for intelligent questions while defense lawyers disagreed.

63. Ranii, *supra* note 62 at 19.

64. Forston, *supra* note 16 at 632; *Taking Note of Note-Taking*, 10 Colum. J. of L. & Soc. Problems 565, 574-77.

65. *See, Taking Note of Note-Taking, supra* note 64.

66. Gerhart continues: "Although two of the judges I interviewed expressed concern that note-taking would distract jurors from listening to the evidence or give a note-taking juror undue influence in jury deliberation, seven of the judges said that permission to take notes, which was permitted in all the jury cases I studied, has been beneficial.... Even in cases where only a few jurors took notes, no bias in jury deliberation has been perceived." *Report on the Empirical Case Studies Project* to the Nat. Com. for the Review of Antitrust Laws and Procedures 65-66 (1979).

67. Patterson v. Colorado, 205 U.S. 454, 462 (1907).

68. Zenith Radio Corp. v. Matsushita Electric Industrial Co., 1979 Trade Cas. 62753 at 78342. *See*, H. Kalven, H. Zeisel, The American Jury 151 (1966); M. Saks, *Small Group Decision Making and Complex Information Tasks*. (Fed. Jud. Center 1981).

69. *See generally*, Wasserman, Robinson, *Extra-Legal Influences, Group Processes, and Jury Decision-Making: A Psychological Perspective*, 12 N.C. Central L.J. 96 (1980).

70. Vinson, *supra* note 36 at 1245. Vinson notes the stress factor created by the restriction:

> At this point one of the most important dynamics of any jury became evident. Jurors are in an artificial, closely controlled environment, which precludes them from interacting in the very areas that, to them, are of social significance. They are jurors, but the very business of being jurors is just what they are not allowed to discuss. Perhaps this can be more clearly understood through an analogy. Suppose that workers on a job were told that they could discuss anything among themselves except their jobs, their work environment, what they were doing, how they were doing it, and how it impacted them or the organization for which they work. It is obvious that this soon would produce a good deal of stress.

Id.

71. Grady, *supra* note 54 at 257.
72. *See*, e.g., A. Elwork, B. Sales, J. Alfini, Making Jury Instructions Understandable (1982).
73. 631 F.2d 1069 (3d Cir. 1980), discussed in Part I, *supra*.